D0036803

MONEY CAN HEAL

"The inspiring story of how the Rudolf Steiner Foundation came to be such an extraordinary pioneer in conscious finance, locally and globally. You will never see money in the same way after reading this ground-breaking book."
— **Hazel Henderson**, author, *Ethical Markets: Growing The Green Economy*

"This book makes clear that Initiatives like RSF need people like Siegfried Finser and his colleagues, not only with a long term perspective but also with a clear understanding what contemporary spiritual knowledge in the field of money means today. Understanding of what it can do in a positive sense is probably the most forceful source for social renewal today"
— **Peter Blom**, Chairman of the Executive Board, Triodos Bank Group, the European leading Social Bank

"Money Can Heal *may seem a paradoxical title, but look at it this way. Scarcity is inherent in life on earth. Most of us human souls, I firmly believe, come to earth because we need to heal ourselves through developing love in conditions of scarcity. Prices, money, and credit are human inventions for dealing with that scarcity. Thus, healing ourselves through working with them is an essential part of our work on earth. In this book, Siegfried Finser, one of the truly great souls I have known, explains how he and his associates at the Rudolf Steiner Foundation have helped people work together in healing ways around money and credit."*
— **Dr. Clopper Almon**, economist

MONEY CAN HEAL

Evolving Our Consciousness

AND THE STORY OF RSF
AND ITS INNOVATIONS IN SOCIAL FINANCE

SIEGFRIED E. FINSER

STEINERBOOKS

2006

STEINER BOOKS
www.steinerbooks.org
AN IMPRINT OF ANTHROPOSOPHIC PRESS, INC.
610 Main Street, Suite 1
Great Barrington, MA, 01230

Copyright © 2006 by SteinerBooks and Siegfried Finser.

All rights reserved. No part of this publication may be
reproduced, stored in a retrieval system, or transmitted
in any form or by any means, electronic, mechanical,
photocopying, recording, or otherwise without
the prior written permission of the publisher.

COVER AND BOOK DESIGN: WILLIAM (JENS) JENSEN

LIBRARY OF CONGRESS CATALOGING-IN-PUBLICATION DATA

Finser, Siegfried E.
  Money can heal : evolving our consciousness : the story of RSF and its inno-
vations in social finance / Siegfried E. Finser.
      p. cm.
  Includes bibliographical references.
  ISBN-13: 978-0-88010-573-6
  ISBN-10: 0-88010-573-9
  1. Money—Psychological aspects. 2. Wealth—Moral and ethical aspects.
3. Social change. 4. Social evolution. 5. Anthroposophy. I. Title. II. Title:
Social finance.

HG222.3.F56 2006
332.401—dc22
                                                            2006034382

Contents

FOREWORD

This book is more than just a book on money; it is a remarkable example of how the author's life of self-development and practice is revealed through this book. In many ways, it's an autobiography—not of the usual type. This is an autobiography of thought, of action, and of will. It demonstrates the great ability of the human spirit to grapple with the phenomenon the world presents to us in a given lifetime, and to transform it through the individuals' capacities of thinking, feeling, and will. This book is a special tribute to the wisdom inherent in the human being (Anthroposophy). Rudolf Steiner coined this word *Anthroposophy* in the very early 1900s. Now, close to a hundred years after his death, Siegfried Finser gives us this remarkable book informed by a life permeated and transformed by the practical application of the core ideas that Steiner developed.

The publication of this book, we believe, will shed much light on the healing power of money for humanity. It explores the wonders of a variety of monetary transactions through real examples easily recognizable by all of us. Siegfried focuses particularly on the world of transactions and how they constitute a vehicle for transformation. This book shows how humanity is experiencing an evolution of consciousness and can take more responsibility for how money moves in our world.

> Mark A. Finser, President and CEO, RSF
> Lynne Twist, Veteran fund-raiser and global activist,
>   author, *The Soul of Money: Reclaiming the Wealth of
>   Our Inner Resources*

INTRODUCTION

THIS IS A time of increased interest in the nature and character of what we call money. For the most part, the books now available either describe the qualities of currency or take a systems point of view. Some books encourage us to take a moral view and propose ethical standards of sufficiency, or they defend the need for alternative currencies such as frequent flyer miles and time dollars.[1] Of special interest are the writings of Edgar S. Cahn, the founder of time banks and time dollars, as well as Bernard Lietaer, who has caused many to reconsider their personal relationships to money through his definition of money as an agreement between parties. You may certainly wish to read *The Soul of Money* by Lynn Twist for its passion and persuasive argument for a different way of dealing with money.

The view expressed in *Money Can Heal* does not conflict with those described in other books, but derives from a simple point: the magic in the transaction. Transaction is not an entirely adequate word, because it implies a one-way current. If this were so, we would have to say that every such event involves two transactions; selling would be one transaction, buying another. I have found that this is not the case. Buying never occurs without selling, nor does selling occur without buying. They are not separate transactions, but together constitute one transaction, and therein lies the wonder of this purely human event. No other creature in nature engages in such a transaction. It is something uniquely human, since it grew out of humanity's social and community life. Whereas animals care for one another and defend their young, they do not create mutual transactions to obtain their needs, and they certainly do not borrow or give in the way I am using the terms. Animals do not have the capacity to invent or use money. We alone of all nature's creatures have created money as the accepted social means for getting what we need and helping one another realize goals.

Therefore, I have taken the point of view that, since all transactions are uniquely human, we owe it to ourselves to imbue every transaction with our full understanding and conscious intentions. We need to comprehend what we are doing, how the ideas, the feelings, and the nature of our will in every financial transaction affect the world order and our social future. Through every transaction we alter our personal lives and the lives of all the future humans on the face of the Earth. What we carry in our consciousness in every transaction has the potential for changing the world. This book is a consciousness-raising exercise that encourages us to take appropriate action.

In the late 1970s, I was asked to serve as treasurer of the Anthroposophical Society in America, a branch of the General Anthroposophical Society founded and inspired by Rudolf Steiner, who inaugurated Waldorf schools, biodynamic farming, a number of therapies, including anthroposophically extended medicine and the art of eurythmy, and many other activities that grew out of what he termed "spiritual science," the introduction of ethical individualism as a world movement. Inherent in ethical individualism is that all human beings have the developing capacity to transform whatever is not yet perfect in themselves and in the world. In other words, the individuality in each of us is growing and will increasingly take responsibility for the lot of humanity and the Earth.

As part of my service as treasurer, I was forced to take a deep interest in the nature of money and its movement. With great interest, I studied Steiner's series of lectures published as *World Economy,* in which he gives startling revelations about the nature of money. I began to realize that money needs our attention as much as philosophy, education, agriculture, the arts, and sciences. My personal relationship to money was changed when I recognized that our monetary system is a reflection of the human being, and that as the human being develops so will our consciousness about money. Thus every transaction I am involved with has new meaning and new potential because of knowing that it is an extension of myself and expresses outwardly what my intentions are.

In 1979 I was asked to participate in bringing three unique bankers from the Gemeinschafts Bank in Bochum, Germany, for a brief tour of the U.S. Ernst Barkoff, Gisela Reuter, and Rolf Kerler visited nine cities and attended many meetings and discussions about money, and Ernst Barkoff gave an incredible series of lectures. He described what he had discovered about the nature of money and explained how it is an exoteric expression of what lives in the soul life of humanity.

My experience with Ernst Barkoff is described in greater detail in section 7. In spite of my limited German vocabulary, that experience allowed me to translate all that Barkoff had to say, because I learned a new way of listening; I became like a small child absorbing everything without any filters. From my years as a teacher, I know that every small child has this capacity to internalize life experiences without filters. How else could we learn to crawl, stand, walk, talk, and think, except through imitation of what is experienced in human society.

I didn't know it at the time, but there was an added benefit when I slipped back into that small child consciousness and absorbed all that Ernst Barkoff poured out in his words. In my defenseless state, I had soaked up ideas and spiritual impulses from this great man that stayed in me as a kind of individualized treasure to call on and consult in the years that followed. It was available to me for many lectures and conversations with clients. It also gave me the courage and the vision needed to found the Rudolf Steiner Foundation.

By 1984, I found collaborators who would, together with me, create the new Rudolf Steiner Foundation now known as RSF. It is a financial services organization that endeavors to bring soul and spirit into financial transactions. We wanted to change the way the world works with money, the way human beings think of money, and the soul qualities that human beings instill into the movement of money, so that it can truly become the purified life-blood of human society. Section 7 of this book describes the story of the RSF and its mission as it relates to the movement of money.

Because most transactions involve the whole human being—thinking, feeling, and willing—I describe life situations throughout the book for us to consider and penetrate with our understanding. I am less interested in monetary theory or economic systems than in the anatomy of this wonderful event we call a transaction. Rather than postulating a theory and constructing an experiment to prove or disprove it, my method is to pry the theory out of the occurrence. Therefore, you will find this book composed of stories and questions that elicit understanding through the events themselves.

An experienced teacher of younger children knows that a good example is a thousand times more valuable than so-called instruction. My math teacher in high school never actually answered a question. He always started with, "Well now, how would we go about working on this; what makes sense to do first?" He was demonstrating clear thinking to us, because he was not so much interested in getting the answer to the problem. He was allowing us to evolve our thinking capacity to be available for all the problems we might confront in life.

For example, when I look at a maple tree I can observe a great deal, such as colors and shapes. To make sense of what I see, however, I need to go beyond my perceptions to the ideas that live in them. The leaves have a flat form with five points of various sizes and are lined with veins through which the sap moves and sustains the form. Do I actually see the five points, the veins, and the living sap? No, I do not. Those parts of my experience are not given to me by my senses. My senses cannot count, but I can because I have the concept of numbers and their interrelationships. I am moving past what I can observe and touching the boundaries of the spirit—what lives behind the sense perceptible and all that I can reveal through my capacity for thinking. My math teacher was revealing the fringes of spirit when he taught me how to think.

I am not an economist, nor am I an accountant. Neither am I a mystic or faithful believer in what most today call spirit. I define spirit as the invisible attribute of visible phenomena that can be experienced and identified through the gifts of human thinking, feeling, and willing. In other words, spirit is everywhere, hidden in matter, to be discovered by us through thinking. I not only seek knowledge, but also wisdom rooted in experience rather than in theory. I am simply, as we all are, a person who has dealt with money for a lifetime and even had to help others deal with money in the context of their life situations. As treasurer of the Anthroposophical Society, I had to learn what is involved in organizational money. I have often had to work with clients on budgeting and projections. Each client's relationship to money is unique, and my advice needed all the imagination I could muster.

Most of this book is derived from the many lectures and articles I have given and written during the last twenty-one years. This is the first opportunity I have had to organize them all into a single coherent statement about the spiritual significance of money. I acknowledge the great debt I owe to Ernst Barkoff for much that I have to say. I also owe much of my personal research and insights to the great thinker, teacher, and artist of the invisible, Rudolf Steiner.

To Rudolf Steiner I owe not only many of the ideas that inspire me, but also a worldview that has given me a sense of mission and purpose. From him and his many translated lectures and books, I first gleaned the concept of the threefold human being: the nerve and sensory aspect, the rhythmic breathing and circulatory aspect, and the metabolic and limb system. He also helped me clarify the differences among thinking, feeling, and willing. The need to distinguish between body, soul, and spirit also dawned on me through reading his many lectures and books.

His very first book, *The Philosophy of Freedom*, took me systematically along a path of inquiry that not only clarified many other philosophies, but also placed them in a context of the developing consciousness of the human being.[2] I spent three years with a group of young people studying that book, meeting once a week to argue and discuss the various points. It turned out to be time well spent that helped me form the bedrock of my worldview.

Finally, through Steiner's descriptions of the evolutionary process of the human being, I began to understand who I was. I was then able to engage in a lifelong conversation with the one angel being out of the spiritual hierarchies who had chosen to accompany my human struggle with wisdom and goodness of purpose.

I have great gratitude for all that is in my biography and the help I received all along the way from relatives, friends, and teachers. I owe much to my wife Ruth, whose unwavering love and support helped me to express myself in words and action. She was at all times a living example of a good human being. I am also grateful to my two sons; Torin Finser, with his scholarly penetration into Rudolf Steiner's thoughts and his imaginative descriptions, gave me the courage to write this book through the example of his own many volumes. Mark Finser united his life with the life of RSF and brought his incredible social gifts to an organism I could only begin but not complete. His deep understanding of the life and soul element emanating from his connection with the spirit of our time brought me endless happiness and confidence in the growth and development of RSF.

I also want to thank the many teachers in the Rudolf Steiner School and High Mowing School for giving me a foundation I could build on. They are too numerous to mention them all, but Beulah Emmet, the founder of High Mowing School, created a place in the universe where someone like me could grow out of childhood into youth with capacities intact and ready to apply to what life would bring me. This book and all it contains arises out of immense gratitude for the biography I was able to create in the company of such benevolent human and other beings. It chronicles the path I took, intellectually and emotionally, to eventually connect money with a healing impulse.

Money Can Heal is a call to the social physicians of every race, religion, nation, gender, and personal persuasion who wish to heal our social life. It is a call to those who want to let their forces stream into the realm of reality in a manner that positively affects our monetary circulation. Just as our body is sustained and healed through the marvelous circulation of our blood, the circulation called money can heal our social life. The circulation of the blood in our body is continually renewed through oxygen, which is taken out of the wide world and integrated into the flow of blood touching all aspects of our being. *The circulation of money is continuously renewed through the penetration of human spiritual initiative and social intentions into it as well.*

As the heart, the seat of feeling and love, gives each of us the motive for living, so the forces of love enter the stream of time through the human being to evolve our wisdom-filled universe into a universe imbued with love.

Human society can become an organism that is sensitive to the finest qualities in human nature. In addition to the stories and examples and the basic information about the way money moves, you will find in this book a few simple exercises that can transform each of us and transform the way money moves and affects the world. I encourage everyone who reads this book to take up the human task of healing the world through money.

IMAGINATION AND MONEY

1. Imaginative Cognition

W̲E USE MONEY every day and assume quite naturally that we know what it is. What can we learn by delving into its deeper meanings? As human beings we are changing all the time through our experiences, our feelings, and the content of our thoughts. All of us are in a process of development. Since money is intimately connected with human social life and is a human invention not found in nature, is it possible that money is also in a process of development? If money is not a mechanical or fixed piece of matter, but linked in its very nature to what the human being is, then it may also imitate human nature in how it functions in society. Because both money and we are constantly developing, it might be that we know only what money *was*, never how it is and will become. All our thoughts are based on what money used to be, and we do not notice how rapidly it is changing. We will see later that money used to be an object, but now it is more of a living stream of movement and will develop even further as we, too, develop.

This book reaches for the nature of money at the edge of its potential metamorphosis over the next few decades and beyond. I am operating on the assumption that what money will one day become is already inherent in its present form. By studying what it is now, we may be able to uncover its potential. We are struggling to see what is not yet visible to our senses and is barely discernible to our thinking. We can easily observe and understand money as an object. Visualizing money as a flow of value that encircles the globe and stimulates human productivity and creativity requires more effort.

By looking into the evolving nature of money, this book encourages us to liberate a capacity we already possess but are just beginning to develop. I call this capacity *imaginative cognition,* or imaginative thinking. The book presents, in anecdotal form, a variety of ordinary monetary experiences that resemble those we encounter in daily life.

Then, using imaginative cognition, we discover a number of truths from our anecdotes.

What does *imaginative cognition* mean? This is not a common term. *Imaginative cognition* means the human ability to picture what is not perceptible to the senses and, in doing so, to connect sense-perceptible phenomena with conceptual images. This imaginative cognition is what we need in order to deal with all the invisible phenomena occurring behind the visible, physical phenomena we are familiar with in daily life. Examples of phenomena that are invisible to us are growth, life, feelings, thoughts, movement, and even progress. We use many such invisible phenomena in our daily discourse.

Let's consider them one at a time. In chapter 2, the concepts of growth and life are discussed. That chapter also discusses the nature of our feelings. Chapter 3 explores the question of human progress, and chapter 4 describes how the use of imaginative thinking is needed to understand the nature of money.

2. Can You See It Grow?

Growth

LET US REGARD a plant as an example of the invisible phenomena of growth. Imagine placing a seed in the dark, moist earth. Take in the wonderful odor of organic material decomposing and becoming soil. Cover the seed and allow it to rest in the mysterious dark soil, within what we can only imagine as a great silence. Now picture the seed expanding and how it is moved to labor silently in the dark. Visualize the shell of the seed beginning to crack and a pale tentacle of root exploring its surroundings. It naturally moves downward further into its home environment.

Shortly thereafter, another shoot emerges from the now wide-open seed and immediately strives upward against gravity, knowingly in search of the light. As it breaks into the light-filled air, the root grows dramatically downward into the earth, counterbalancing the upward effort of the shoot. Every day when we look at the plant, it is different. It has extended itself farther into the air toward the sun. Unfolding leaf after leaf, the plant arises from the ground.

At a given moment the growth upward seems to halt, and at the tips of the plant it bunches as if assembling new forces for the next step. The leaves that are bunched now swell, become a bud, and then burst open into glorious color. The plant has reached an apex of some sort. It has revealed its ultimate nature, transformed from root to stem to leaf to flower, within which the seed develops for another life cycle. Our senses give us all of this information—or do they?

Do we really *see* it grow with our eyes? We see it only at different stages at different times. In the blink of an eye, the plant may have changed. We take note of this new perception, connect it with our last perception, and associate the difference with what we know as "growth." In our imagination, we connect what we saw yesterday with what we see today and, finding a host of concepts we have acquired since childhood, actually feel that we *see* the growth occurring in front of our eyes. *Growth*, like *life* is not observable with our senses, but through imaginative thinking we can connect stages of growth and come close to an experience of what it is, but not just through our senses. Our creative and imaginative thinking gives us a tangible experience of growth.

This aspect of our thinking should not be confused with fantasy or subjective creativity. If we base our pictures solely on what delights or pleases us, we can develop wonderful and fantastic pictures. Even cartoons sometimes depict something quite arbitrary and subjective. Imaginative cognition is not fantasy; it is a tool that helps us understand the world and ourselves. Other examples of invisible phenomena uncovered by imaginative cognition are life and what we call feelings. Let's first consider life.

WE THINK WE ARE ALIVE.

All that is alive, moves, changes, or is transformed can be observed only in its various stages. We cannot actually see life or the acts of change and transformation. Only our faculty of thinking can connect the various perceptions we have and unite them with acquired concepts into a whole that lets us experience the nature of *life*.

William Wordsworth offers an expression of this experience in the last verse of his poem, *The Daffodils:*

> For oft, when on my couch I lie,
> In vacant or in pensive mood,
> They flash upon that inward eye,
> Which is the bliss of solitude:
> And then my heart with pleasure fills,
> And dances with the daffodils.

What was his "inward eye?" True, a memory was recalled, but with what eyes did he see that memory or any other memory? What eyes do we have that search inwardly for pictures that can fill us with joy or loathing or envy or a myriad of other emotions? These eyes also picture the world in which we live and connect all our perceptions into a whole experience that is intelligible to us. This is the eye that perceives and pictures concepts; it complements and even completes what the world presents to us through our senses.

With this imaginative aspect of our thinking, we are able to behold concepts similar to the way our eye permits us to see colors. While we observe the physical world with our senses, we are able to perceive the conceptual world at the same time and connect the two. With our thinking capacity, we bridge a world that is given to us, divided into the visible through our senses and the invisible made visible through our capacity to picture the invisible. In other words, we see the material world with our senses and the spiritual part of the world with our thinking. While we perceive all that is perceptible with our senses, including eyes, ears, skin, and taste, we connect our varied perceptions through our ability to picture their associations in concepts and mental images. We might say that, through our thinking, we see the intervals and relationships that are invisible to our senses.

We will later see that the concepts we have about money cause us to miss some of its main invisible features, thus getting stuck in the idea that money is an object, a thing subject only to physical forces. It is the purpose of this book to awaken creative, imaginative thinking, a capacity we all have, through which we can experience *growth* and *life* and then apply it to the medium of money and its movement.

When we experience our feeling life, which is so important to all of us, our everyday thinking cannot quite place our feelings into the reality of existence. Are our feelings objectively real or real for us only as subjective phenomena? As rational beings, we are expected to assess our feelings as subjective, meaning they have no objective reality. Consequently, our feelings are important only to *us,* and we expect to be able to hide them effectively so that no one in the world will really know them. Naturally, if we express them through words, gestures, or actions, others may become aware of what we think of as our inmost, private feelings. The feelings themselves, without any outer expression, are deemed not to affect the *real* world in any objective, measurable way.

Edward Lee Thorndike's 1910 work on quantitative methods, *Educational Psychology,* famously reformulates an idea originally stated by René Descartes, "Anything that exists must exist to some extent, and therefore it can be measured, weighed, or counted."[1] In other words, to exist, anything qualitative must be reduced to its quantitative nature to be considered real. Hence, because our feeling life is composed exclusively of qualitative rather than quantitative substances, it doesn't really exist since none of it can be measured, weighed, or counted.

The idea that our feelings are subjective and merely private to each of us is a falsely indoctrinated conclusion that doesn't match our actual experience. As people wake up to their inner life, they increasingly understand that feelings are not just subjective and personal, but are very much an aspect of the reality we experience and thus form an objective part of the world. It is just that, through our feelings, we experience the same objective world reality in a different way; it affects us more directly. It has direct, inner impact on us and reveals qualitative aspects not available through the senses. In a way, we are more connected to the objective world through our feelings than we are through our senses, because to observe the world we have to remove ourselves and see it at a distance before the senses can work properly. With our feelings, we remain more connected, more involved, and less separate. That's why our feelings engage us and can overwhelm us. The sight of a beautiful sunset or the sound of a stirring symphony can move us to tears.

Everywhere, we observe not only the verbal expressions of what others feel and think, but we also note how the driving forces in most human actions and counteractions are inner feelings and thoughts. For example, how often do first impressions linger and eventually blossom into full-blown judgments? Sometimes we are wrong in our first impressions, but more often than not they end up guiding our interactions. That is precisely what differentiates human beings from the entire animal world; our actions are determined largely by the motives we arrived at and through the thoughts and feelings that move us to activity. We may be able to take a philosophical position that our feelings and thoughts are subjective and not real, but simple observation of life concludes otherwise.

Marriage, for example, is only an outer expression of love. If the underlying love is not a reality, how could we manage the many years of ups and downs of living together? If we need to take a reasonable position in life, we will make a mistake in dismissing the feelings and thoughts that drive our social actions. They may not be measurable, but they do exist and live not only in us, but also between us. Love between two people is a constant work of art that both individuals create through living together, and it exists as long as they both renew it in every moment of their time together. The underpinnings of a strong marriage exist when both parties continue to create and develop. A marriage between two people is representative of the social actions that occur in our larger world. Can we develop and progress or are we stuck in what we are?

3. Are We Progressing?

To bring a healing impulse into the movement of money we need to consider whether human beings develop and are able to transform themselves into people with better qualities and attributes. Progress without our participation seems futile. We are too conscious and too willful to be bystanders in our own development.

As a rule, we tend to think of *progress* in terms of specific physical improvements in our diet, work place, physical condition, and especially longevity. We believe human progress will eventually result in a kind of paradise on Earth. If things are to improve, they must improve physically. Improving our civilization seems to mean having more and better quality food, increasing comfort in living conditions, and obliteration of pain and suffering. Our age sees reality as physical, and improvement as a consequence of something physical. If we drive this point of view to its conclusion, we end up believing that we will someday live for eternity without pain or suffering and in perfect health. Is that the ultimate achievement? The fact that death is as much a part of existence as is life does not enter the equation.

What about progress in terms of how and what we are? What about developing ourselves into better beings than we are? Is that possible? What would it be like to find something within ourselves that has yet to be developed? What would our lives together be like if we helped each other develop new capacities that are presently dormant in each of us? If we did not leave our future to accident but had a vision of ourselves in future centuries that included growth in such qualities as compassion, love, and responsibility—what would that look like?

All of life is a kind of school, which helps us organize and make sense of our existence. It also embalms us in a conceptual framework, however, that often prevents us from confronting new experiences without the filters we have learned to apply to them. When I walk

with friends and we pass a neighbor's front garden alive with color-
ful plants in full bloom and bees and butterflies busy in their hom-
age, invariably someone will name the plants as bee balm or asters
or echinacea. We feel a great sense of relief once we have identified a
perception, and now all is well with the world. However, tagging the
name onto a beautiful flower does not enhance our enjoyment very
much. On the contrary, the name seems of slightly lesser value than
the perception itself.

Why is it that we so quickly name everything we experience? Do
we know something better when it has the name? Just think how we
go around labeling everything a small child encounters, as if the name
is what matters, not the experience. Have you ever seen a small child
crouched over a tiny flower or a hermit crab at the beach? The child
hovers over the phenomena, absorbing its every detail, soaking it up
like a sponge and wrapping it inwardly into a remembered treasure.

A name is a concept. It isn't the flower itself. It is a label we have
added to our perceptions to order the existence of something in our
framework of concepts. When we do that, we feel great comfort in
knowing that we have disposed of the unknown so efficiently. We not
only bring concepts to our perceptions, but we also integrate every perception into an edifice of concepts. The concept of violet connects with
the concept of plant, leaves, color, growth, sunshine, and water. They
form an endless structure of connecting concepts that integrate to form
a whole worldview. Whenever a new experience comes to us, we rush
to integrate it into the existing network of concepts. If we cannot do
this, we sometimes force it, hide parts of the raw experience, or paper
it over with what we already know. Rarely do we alter the network of
concepts, because it is too uncomfortable to do that. To reorganize our
whole network of concepts makes us feel, literally, as though our world
is falling down around our ears.

Whether human beings are progressing or not needs to be looked
at from a fresh perspective. It would be difficult to maintain that
we are progressing if we find no evidence that we have already progressed in the past. I explore this question more deeply in section
six, because it is related to our interest in money. I maintain that we
have progressed and are in the process of continuing to develop, but

money, too, accompanies our development and changes to match our new condition. When I bring imaginative thinking to bear on my perceptions about money, I bring a fresh approach to them, and find that new qualities are revealed. Not only do we have to acknowledge what we already know, but also we have to investigate what we do not yet know.

4. MONEY IS …

IF WE ARE to study the true nature of money, we need to reassess some of our concepts about money and dare to think fresh thoughts. We can apply our imaginative thinking to our personal experiences of money. We can use the same imaginative cognition that gives us experiences of *life, growth, feelings, thoughts, movement,* and *progress* to our experiences with money to reach a fuller understanding of its nature.

It is quite natural to regard money as a physical thing. After all, we are most familiar with currency—the paper money and coins—we use to purchase small items. We imagine it moving around the world as a flood of things. We expect that having it can be a cumulative quantity and aggregate the way all physical things do. When you place a brick on top of three others, you begin to have a pile. That's just how things behave in the world of physical objects. Who ever heard of looking at money any differently?

The truth is that money is less a thing, less an object, and more of a world circulatory movement that responds and enhances our human spiritual life, of which our feelings and ideas are only the tip of the iceberg. This movement touches all human beings, draws the fruits of their activity into circulation, discharges them for consumption, and remains untouched by the physical forces that move objects in space. Like the blood in our bodies, it not only maintains life but also removes illness and suffering, empowers us to accomplish our intentions, and enhances the community of living organisms.

Money, which first dawned on human consciousness as a coin, has evolved from being an object to being sheer movement. Suppose it is only an object when it is not in circulation, when it is not money? Further, suppose it is only money when it is in motion and involved in a transaction? Can we perceive money in the way it slows down, speeds up, and eddies in pools, and rushes around the globe in pure response to human intentions? Can it be youthful, grow elderly, be a bit sickly, or even die? These questions arise when we consider money not as a thing but as a worldwide living force, unleashed and given purpose and meaning by human beings at their various stages of development. In order to view money as movement, we will need to apply imaginative cognition to our own personal experiences with money.

Let us begin our study with a brief reminder of the history of money. A more thorough account of this can be found in, among other sources, *The History of Money* by Jack Weatherford or *A History of Money* by Glyn Davies.[2] Let us look into mythology for the earliest indications of transactions. Then we will review the appearance of barter and the first coins, how coins began to blend with precious metals, later were separated from them, and eventually began to become the world circulation now operating in our economic system.

5. A Few Historical Reminders

Secular Roots

In *Norse Myths,* in the story "The Doom of Loki and his Children," the gods can no longer control Fenris, the terrible wolf child of Loki. They decide that only a magic chain can subdue him.

> Whereupon the messenger of the Vans, Skrynir, who knew the land of the Swartheim, was dispatched with presents and promises to the Dwarf King, and he, when he heard the gods' request, thought for a while with pursed lips and wrinkled brow.

> "Yes," he said at length, "it may be done. Wait here for three days and at the end of that time the chain shall be ready."[3]

The idea of exchanging goods or services is not the prevalent way of obtaining what is needed in these ancient tales. The gifts and promises brought to the Dwarf King were intended to make him more receptive to the request. It was not a payment or an exchange, nor did the gods purchase or barter for their needs. In this early culture described in the *Norse Myths,* and in many other legendary episodes, giving and receiving preceded buying and selling or even exchanging. The myths and oral tradition, our earliest evidence, point to the transaction of giving/receiving.

It requires a particularly modern mind-set to demand equal exchange for a service or an object. Before barter could exist, the concepts of fairness and value parity needed to exist. It is impossible to exchange objects without a clear sense of the worth of both objects. Imagine yourself in an exchange or barter situation. Would you exchange eighty-five eggs for a handful of rice? Would that seem fair? The concept of fairness or parity of value had to exist in our consciousness before an exchange was possible. Even though it is hard to establish the value of any object, the "exchangers" needed to feel that what was exchanged was of relative equal value. Bartering needed a consciousness that included *value, fairness, exchanging,* and *trust.*

Probably, with the beginning of agricultural and craft activity, the transactions of exchange or barter also came into being. This practice appears to predate any historical records and recedes into a time so far back that we are not able to identify its beginning. What I refer to as the secular roots of money grew out of the practice of living in community. Barter requires a recognition that differences exist among us in skills and needs. It also requires an understanding that our needs can be met by exchanging very different objects or services that we agree have relatively equal value. A gift to our neighbor is not yet barter. Only when we put a *value* on our gift and expect something of equal value in return does barter begin. It is our expectation of parity in exchange that determines whether something is a gift or a bartered item.

It is unlikely that our ancestors thought out barter conceptually. More than likely, it was practiced under the guidance of accepted leadership. It may actually have required the presence of a third party or the family patriarch, matriarch, or tribal chief to ensure that the exchange took place under fair conditions.

It is unknown how long pure barter was practiced before subtle changes in the exchange dynamics appeared. Nearly all consumable commodities, such as tobacco, chocolate, grain, dried fish, and fruits, served to facilitate the exchange of values at one time or another and at one geographical location or another. The exchange of *consumable* commodities for *durable* commodities no doubt became common simply out of the practice and the desire to lengthen the time when values were sustained. For example durable commodities such as cloth, furs, feathers, whale teeth, boar tusks, or shells served better, since they simply endured for a longer time. However, these all occurred naturally and, as a result, each object was unique and its value was difficult to appraise. Even the cowry shell, which was popular across much of Africa, was of no use to most people in the world. Because other peoples did not see its value, the shells always had limited circulation in specific areas.

As Paul Einzig states, "Money never exists in a cultural or social vacuum. It is not a mere lifeless object but a social institution."4 In other words, to operate as money, a material cannot exist simply as an object; it requires the presence of a particular social and cultural system. Any object that begins to assume the function of money must grow out of a cultural reference. It must function within a network of social agreements and understandings.

SACRED ROOTS

In contrast to the secular roots of money, the sacred roots of money actually predate our earliest records of barter agreements. The first known coin in historical records appears in Sumatra around 3,000 BC. One who delivered a quantity of grain to the temple of Inanna-Ishtar, the goddess of life, death, and fertility, would receive a coin, or "shekel," which stood for a measure of grain roughly equivalent to a bushel. The coin entitled such individuals to return at a time of their choosing to claim certain services from the temple. It is believed that the nature of those services was sexual and that the priestesses were trained and skilled in their delivery. Viewed from the perspective of our twenty-first-century consciousness, we cannot fully comprehend the spiritual nature of the agreement between the temple and the individual. At that time, all the normal routines and events of life were carefully regulated by the priests and priestesses of such temples.

The coin itself, dating about 3000 BC, was a bronze piece with an image of a sheaf of grain being surrendered to the priestess, with the likeness of the goddess on the other side. The important aspect of these early transactions is not what was exchanged, but that the coin facilitated an exchange. The coin represented a right that was retained by the owner of the physical coin and could not be separated from it. Whoever possessed the coin had the right to exchange it. We will consider later what a *right* is and how it relates to the movement of money, but for now it is sufficient to say that the coin was a physical object that signified a human right guaranteed by the temple of its origin.

It is as though the right, something non-physical, something purely social, was crystallized into the shekel. As salt is crystallized out of a liquid state, the coin was crystallized out of the social realm of human agreements.

Why ideas and certain practices occur at certain times in human history is a mystery. Why did coinage not appear earlier in human civilization? Why around 3000 BC? Some historians and sociologists offer explanations that transport our modern consciousness back into early times to find logical reasons for how something came about. This makes it sound as though those earlier human beings were just as we are today, deriving their practices from physical needs, which were met through the application of logic.

Unfortunately the concept of logic did not appear in history until somewhat later, during the time of ancient Greece when philosophy became prominent. Many of us picture twenty-first century people, with our modern consciousness, trudging about the world 5,000 years ago, carrying their belongings and telling themselves, "There's got to be a better way." Moreover, after giving it some thought, they then came to the wonderful idea of a coin or, say, a wheel. An even more naïve explanation is offered, which sees coins coming about accidentally. We imagine someone sees a tumbleweed driven along by the wind. "Ah ha!" says that twenty-first century person, transported to 5,000 years ago, "Round things roll, and if we connect a few together and push we will have a cart, which will save us much labor." In the case of the coin, the shekel was an inspired idea, and at that time priests and priestesses were specially trained from childhood on to receive inspirations. It appears that the first known coin in human history was associated with a spiritual revelation to a particular religious organization dwelling in an established temple.

We would love to believe that the beginnings of money came about through the intelligence of some shrewd businessperson who grasped the significance of money for the future and deliberately compelled the brain to bring forth the bright idea of a coin. This reinforces our naïve view that ancient human beings were no different than we are today in how we think and act—just dumber, less perceptive, and more superstitious. An alternative way to regard the history of humankind is to take at face value the myths, sagas, songs, literature, and art, whose remnants remain for study. Why not accept what they give as evidence and conclude that people grew from a somewhat childlike consciousness, being guided and tutored by superhuman leaders who directly served spiritual beings ranking above them. Over long periods of development, the self-aware, intelligence-based thinking of our age come into being.

The history of humanity is the history of a being in process, first manipulated and guided largely by spiritual beings, and then gradually becoming more independent and self-regulating. The life of an individual follows this same pattern, growing from baby to child, then to teen to young adult, and finally to a responsible self-motivating independent being among other adults. The evolution of money parallels the later development of the human being. It, too, has changed from coin to an association with precious metals to the connection with economic vitality of a nation and then to credit and now to sheer worldwide circulatory motion. Money is on the cusp of another change as it becomes increasingly sensitive to the human soul and spirit. It can act almost as a panacea for social and physical ills. Human beings have developed far enough to invest the movement of money with a healing impulse.

THE TRANSACTION OF BUYING AND SELLING

6. JOHN'S BARGAIN

LOST IN AN unfamiliar neighborhood, John stops at a school to ask for directions. The sign on the building says "Waldorf School." From the outside, the building looks ordinary. School is not in session, and he does not hear the sounds of children in the building. He has never heard of Waldorf schools before, but he guesses somebody must be around who will know his destination and give him directions.

There is no one in the hallway and John wanders along the hall looking at the artwork of the children. He passes a display case filled with handwork completed by the students in the various grades and admires the skill and artistic sense exhibited.

The door to a classroom is next to the case, and he wanders in looking for someone to help him. He moves past the rows of children's desks and chairs toward the front of the room. A large desk obviously belonging to the teacher is off to the left side of the room to provide a complete view of all activities in the room. Although the room is silent, he imagines what it is like when the room is filled with children.

Behind and to the side of the teacher's desk is another smaller desk that catches his eye. It is obviously old, not yet antique, and perhaps even handmade by an amateur carpenter. The facing folds down to provide a writing space. It is closed and conceals any contents. John pulls down the facing to its flat position. The desk is empty. Not even a pencil can be seen. John slides open one of the small drawers, and it, too, is empty. He tries another. Empty! Maybe the desk isn't used by anyone.

Something about this desk stirs his memory. He remembers one like this in his room high on the top floor of his parents' old house. It couldn't be! The same maple finish, three large drawers below, and the same cast iron pulls on the drawers. There's one way to find out. John reaches in behind the two small drawers inside the desk. With his index finger he searches and finds a small button the size of a nail head. He pulls gently on the button. Soundlessly a small flat door opens revealing a hidden chamber. He reaches inside to find it empty. Perhaps the owner doesn't even know it is there.

John knows what it used to contain. All his secret treasures, things he didn't want anyone to know about. His secret hiding place for things he considered private. This is not his desk, but it is exactly like the one that he had in his room as a child. A desire to own it again comes over him.

"May I help you?" The voice is behind him. He surreptitiously closes the secret panel before turning around. At the door, a woman in business attire with a pleasant face regards him, questioning his presence.

"Hello," says John, "I came in looking for someone to give me directions, and then noticed this desk."

"Oh, that old thing," laughs the stranger. "It's been in the school for years. It's too small for a teacher and not right for a student."

"I like it," says John. "Are you someone I can talk to about buying it? Although I notice it has seen better days and is chipped here and there, I would like to purchase it. I am sure the school would welcome an opportunity to purchase a newer, more functional desk to replace it."

"Well, I appreciate the interest, but that desk was made by a former teacher of the school and we use it all the time. I'm the administrator of the school, and I can tell you it's not for sale. Can I help you with directions?"

"Thank you, that's very kind of you. What would you say the desk is worth," John asks.

The administrator replies, "I have no idea and it's not for sale."

"I would value it and take good care of it," John interrupts. "Would the school consider $200? I am sure it is not really worth that much, but it is exactly like the one I had as a boy. It has sentimental value for me."

The administrator responds, "I'm sorry, but it's not for sale, and we also treasure it for its sentimental value. The woodwork teacher who made it was very well liked, and his memory is connected with that desk. I'm sure you can find another desk to your liking."

John then suggests, "Suppose I was to offer $300 for it; do you think the school could find a replacement for it?"

"I am sure the school could," says the administrator, "but you see we need it and treasure it and couldn't sell it."

"It doesn't seem to be used. The teacher already has a much larger and better desk to use. Are you sure it can't be spared?" John continues, "And, even though I know full well that I could obtain a brand new desk with all the drawers I need for much less than $300, I am willing to pay as much as $500 for it."

At this point the school administrator seriously considers that the school is short of funds, is struggling to keep to its balanced budget, and begins to wonder whether $500 might not be enough to purchase a new desk and add the proceeds to the cash flow. Then she realizes the desk is precious to everyone and it would be difficult to justify her decision on the matter.

"No," she says, "I'm sorry, even $500 would not compensate for its value to us."

John senses a note of indecision. He also notices the phrasing in the answer and realizes what was a closed issue is now open for negotiation. Some of this is quite conscious, but some is more instinctive. His desire for the desk is now palpable.

John then continues, "I have already offered much more than I should, but I also don't want to short change the school in any way. Much against my better judgment, I would like to make a final offer of $700, and I hope you realize how very fair this offer is."

The administrator does realize how fair it is. She knows she can acquire a very utilitarian secondhand desk for about $100 and realizes that she may be lauded for striking such a good bargain. After all, at the annual auction, many treasured objects belonging to the school and the parents have been sold for much less to bring in supplementary funds for support. She decides the right decision is to sell the desk.

With that thought she says, "Well, reluctantly, for the sake of the school's financial condition, we are willing to sell the desk for $800."

John realizes they are now negotiating. "Would you consider $750?

The administrator pauses, thinks it over, and then says, "All right."

The details are quickly settled, a check is exchanged, and the proud new owner leaves with the desk, entirely satisfied that he has purchased something of great value to him. When he recalls the many hours he spent as a boy at just such a desk, the books he read, the papers he composed, the notes he wrote and then hid in the secret compartment, he rejoices over his decision. In his excitement he forgets to ask for directions, but finds his way after all.

When John arrives home, he shows the desk to his wife, Janet. She admires it and asks how much it cost. When he tells her that he paid $750 for it, she is horrified! Janet tells him that he has paid dearly for a whim or, at best, a fond memory out of the past. She exclaims, "I could have gotten you one that may be not so beautiful, but even more functional and certainly tastefully constructed for about $150!"

John is not discouraged. He explains that he had a desk very much like this one and why it is precious to him. He does not mention the secret panel because he prefers that to remain his own special secret place.

In the meantime, the administrator at the Waldorf school quickly replaces the desk with a new one and explains how it happened. After considerable criticism from the faculty for trading a school treasure for a short-term monetary gain, she adds $600 to the school's income amid applause from the finance committee.

That is how John acquired his $750 desk, which he brags about to all his somewhat skeptical friends, and how the Waldorf school substituted an heirloom desk for a manufactured version and some instant cash.

⟶▶ ◀⟵

Although I constructed this story to illustrate certain qualities of money and our relationship to them, I am sure we recognize in it everything we normally experience when we are engaged in buying or selling something. We will take a deeper look at all aspects of this little transaction to see if we can uncover what really happened and any hidden significance that we miss in the reading of the story.

Consider these questions. Do we know or understand what really happened? For example what are the qualities of this particular type of transaction, and what characterizes the exchange of values? To answer these questions we will look a little deeper into the nature of this type of transaction by highlighting some characteristics of money while investigating the nature of the transaction of buying/selling.

7. A COINCIDENCE

I N "JOHN'S BARGAIN" there appears to be a series of accidents or coincidences that lead John into the school and into the large room where
he just happens to see the desk and meet up with the school administrator. He could just as easily stopped at a gas station or convenience
store for directions. Why the school? I generally don't go into a large
building for directions, do you? Perhaps John doesn't either—as a
rule. This time, he did. What impelled him to stop at this place this
time, when ordinarily he might not? What attracted him to admire the
crafts in a glass case down the hallway? How is it that he turned into
the large room where the desk was located, instead of rushing toward
some kind of office? Isn't it remarkable that the administrator, the one
person in the school able to transact a sale with him, should happen to
come into the room and see him admiring the desk?

In a way, these questions pertain mostly to the human situation
before the actual transaction takes place. We want to focus on the
nature of the transaction itself. However, when we contemplate how
much of our life seems accidental and how much of what we encounter is coincidence, it can fill us with wonder. It is as though we sense
something other than our own consciousness at play in our actions and
decisions. Is it possible that there are unseen powers concealed in the
background of our lives?

Consider how often we act on a whim or without a solid reason.
As rational beings, we appear to be very selective about when to be
rational. Most of us have good reasons for less than ten percent of our
decisions. For the rest, we may as well toss a coin. Think of the millions of minor decisions we make every day, choosing a route to the
office, deciding whom to phone first, forgetting or not forgetting to
take something with us that changes the day and our lives. How often
do you think: If I hadn't missed that traffic light, I wouldn't have had to
catch the next train, where I met Alfred for the first time. Alternatively,
you might wonder: If I had remembered my shopping list, I wouldn't

have cruised up and down the aisles and stumbled over a knocked down can of coffee, spraining my ankle. The thousands of little decisions seem to lead us unwittingly into situations or to avoid others we don't even know about.

Whatever causes us to do one thing or another is not revealed immediately. Even our apparent reasonableness often contains hidden motives or other forces. For example, my roommate at college fell in love with a beautiful girl. They were both just nineteen years old, and family and friends all argued in favor of waiting to marry until they had both completed college and could reasonably be expected to have jobs and a way to support themselves. I was present when he tried to make a rational decision. He ruled a piece of paper with two columns. As a heading for one column he wrote *Reasons to Wed*. Heading up the other column he wrote *Reasons to Wait*. Then he thought a bit and began to list various reasons, each under the appropriate heading. When he occasionally seemed stuck, I couldn't resist helping him out with a couple of reasons. I tended to favor whichever column was falling behind on the list. After some time, the reasons to wed were still equal to the reasons to wait, even though I kept adding the reasons to wait. He was struggling hard to come up with more reasons to wed whenever I got ahead of him.

Finally he said, "But I love her!"

"That's a good reason to kiss her, but is it a good reason to marry her now?" I replied.

"I don't care," he said. "I'm going to marry her now."

I remember this episode vividly as an example of a friend trying hard to make a rational decision, when all along there were determining factors that outweighed any of his intellectual reasons. Isn't it that way about many of our decisions? Sometimes the real causes in us or outside of us are revealed to us either right away or in the course of time.

I have another friend who went to England to study agriculture at Emerson College. He enjoyed his studies immensely and was determined to return to the United States to somehow buy a farm and grow biodynamic-organic produce. He wanted to contribute to the sustainability of the Earth. Within the first month, however, he met a girl who was studying art. She was very creative and talented, alive and dynamic, and she awoke new interests and capacities in him. She persuaded my friend to take a role in a Shakespeare play being performed by an actors group at the college. He turned in a wonderful performance and liked it. Soon after they moved to London together, they were married. She painted and did rather well at an exhibit for her benefit. He enrolled in an acting studio and began his performing career. Later on, I was present for the christening of their third child.

Now, objectively, but with an open mind, look at the circumstances of the lives I have just described. What really motivated my friend to go to England for his agricultural training? We like to think that what governs our lives is our ability to form goals and achieve them. Yet frequently the motive that leads to particular actions appears to be hidden from us. We seem to live among effects of causes not clearly known to us. Isn't it possible that coincidence may contribute to many of our financial transactions as well? The story of "John's Bargain" includes coincidence as contributing *accidentally* to John's finding his beloved desk. If he hadn't stopped at the school, if he hadn't turned into that particular classroom, or if the administrator hadn't seen him and accosted him, all might have turned out different.

Anyone wondering how money can become a healing force in human society has to deal with such questions eventually. Our lives are filled with unanswered questions, mysterious occurrences, and generous guidance from both known and unknown sources. Those with a bit of feeling for the wonder of their lives must eventually confront what has happened to them owing to non-rational influences. Later, we will see that even the movement of money is influenced in this way. We will see that, just as in the story of "John's Bargain," every transaction is open to some kind of accidental intervention that aids or hinders its consummation. As you become more sensitive to such influences, you can begin to look for them in your next few transactions.

When we say something occurred "accidentally" or as a "coincidence," we think we have found the cause for the given incident, whereas in reality we have only named some unknown cause. Our perceptions, without further thinking, do not permit seeing the causes of events directly. Even when an obvious event occurs, such as a stone falling from the edge of a roof, we hypothesize, perhaps suggesting that it was the wind. The immediate cause is apparent for physical occurrences. However, why was the wind so strong at that place? We can go on asking why for quite some time without feeling certain that we have discovered the root cause. At some point, we decide to stop asking why and accept whatever point we have reached. Why not accept that, if there are sense-perceptible causes, there are also super-sensible causes not available to the senses, which we cannot observe until we have developed additional organs of perception: creative, imaginative thinking?

For any source to be a root cause, it must originate from a primary force; in other words, it must be independently willed. In the case of "John's Bargain," he might never have purchased the desk at such a seemingly high price if he hadn't been filled with the pleasant memories of his youth. His memory of experiences from long ago intervened in what he considered a reasonable transaction. He was aware of this influence and knew it affected his decision, and decided for it. Had he not known what motivated him, he would have been under its influence and not free. In this case he could honestly consider himself a root cause of his actions.

If a financial transaction or any action is not truly self-willed, then its cause must be outside our consciousness. This can be outside in the world or internally within our own nature. In either case we cannot regard ourselves as the root cause of any such action. If we are unable to be the root cause of any action or event, how do we become responsible for our own evolution and the evolution of the Earth? We must find a way to take charge of ourselves if we want to bring healing into the world we live in.

If we have not thought this through and arrived at approximately such a conclusion, we are forced to believe in a never-ending chain of interlocking causes, mindlessly stretching back through time and encircling the universe. If we really want to understand a root cause, we would have to first review how we determine our own actions, whether we are able to do so freely, and whether we comprehend and oversee what motivates us. In the end we will have to admit that even our own so-called free actions, usually end up being determined by something we were not aware of or something deep within our own unconscious concerns.

It may very well be that most root causes are non-physical and originate in locations other than the world of objects. Just as John's impulse to purchase the desk stemmed from a memory and not from a present need, many apparent causes are not immediately visible. I have long ago concluded that the world of physical objects cannot initiate any actions at all. To bring about any physical activity always requires a non-physical originating force whose effects are in the object world we live in. In other words, we live with our daily consciousness in a world of effects, not causes. For example, when I walk, as I do daily, I wonder why I am taking this route and not that; but I take it anyway, open to what may happen. When I come to a decision about an investment, I explore all the necessary information and advice I can find, and then I find myself leaning either for or against it. I then make a decision, still wondering why. I have to act in all the various realms of my life, and I have to act decisively. There is a difference between fooling myself that I am one hundred percent conscious of my motives and reasons, and knowing that in all instances there are always some unknown influences working on me while I pretend to be fully rational. I can live with this openness to the unknown, because the unknown is the way the world challenges me to employ my imaginative thinking to discover deeper causes in all I experience and do.

8. The Incarnation of Spirit

ALL DURING JOHN'S transaction, the attention of both parties was drawn to the desk. The buyer was interested in every detail of its construction, appearance, texture, age, and utility. Although he had to deal with the seller in order to consummate the transaction, his focus was clearly on the object he hoped to purchase.

Although there are several different types of monetary transactions, this transaction, at least, has the effect of drawing the attention of the parties into the world of objects. The consciousness of the individuals involved was drawn down into the material world in order to transact this bit of business. *Purchasing draws people into the world. It is a transaction that incarnates the human spirit into the world of things.* If being born can be said to draw us into the world, purchasing furthers our downward direction from birth onward.

In a typical shopping mall, we see older as well as younger people. The elderly are often focused more on exercise than on shopping. The middle-aged group with their families are involved in shopping for a family member or for a home being built, outfitted, or furnished. They are there because it is necessary. The teenagers and young adults are the only ones who seem to enjoy what's going on. They love the atmosphere, the focus on things and sounds, and the many people intent on buying or at least looking at things. Moreover, why shouldn't they? After all, teenagers are on their way into the world. They are in the process of incarnating into their bodies and into their life stories. Of course they enjoy the atmosphere in the meccas of consumerism. For them it's almost a religious experience to be engaged in buying and selling. In fact, it's thrilling even to experience it vicariously. Buying and selling is the economic force that draws the human being into incarnation. It is the modern way, via finance, to be lured into existence and to be drawn into life as a participant.

In later years, most of us still feel this force whenever the opportunity to buy something stirs us into action. Perhaps we have a sock with a hole in it. In our hearts, we feel the pull to shop. We may put aside a number of other important activities or projects we should be doing in favor of shopping. The new pair of socks assumes a high priority, even though we still have several pair and could easily wait another few weeks. No, today seems the right time to buy a new pair.

In the spring, when it's time to clean up the garden and get it ready for the summer, even before we weed and rake and bag the winter debris, we suddenly have the urge to drive to the garden center. We buy plants, seeds, mulch, a few tools, and that new bird feeder we saw advertised. By the time we return home we are exhausted from the effort, but satisfied that now we have what we need to get the job done—tomorrow! The buying appears to help us get ourselves together for the project. It incarnates us into our bodies. Yes, all of our lives we feel the pull of buying in our gut as an elemental force, as a financial surrogate for the will to live.

9. It Takes Two

I DECIDE THAT SOMETHING I already own should be sold, but then I change my mind and decide to buy it from myself. The exchange of money from one pocket to the other, and the transfer of the object from a higher shelf to a lower shelf, is a non-transaction. It never shows up in the economy and is meaningless. Buying an object is not something any of us can do alone, whether in our study or on the street. Selling is also something nobody can do in isolation. It takes two of us! It is a mysterious occurrence in which polarity generates movement and value. The healthy tension between the two parties engenders life and meaning.

How many activities do we know that can be done only between two parties? I visited a dance recently and was amazed at how many people appeared to be dancing alone, only occasionally gesturing toward a possible partner. The medical profession is working very hard to make it possible for one person to have children without the benefit of love. Even conversation is dissolving into email messages or text messaging. We send these messages without the benefit of any non-verbal reactions. Much of our social life seems to be about being individuals only loosely associated with others. Yet we certainly congregate when we have the chance. Thirty-five thousand of us may hoot and scream together at a game. A band has the power to draw thousands into concert. We are complex beings, tending increasingly toward isolation while simultaneously being drawn into large crowds. Perhaps they both offer us equal safety and the avoidance of serious interactions. What cannot be done alone are agreements and contracts. By their very nature and practice, they require two parties. A contractual agreement requires two parties, and sometimes even a third party is needed to testify and notarize that the two parties involved are in fact legitimate.

Marriage is also something no one does alone—at least not yet. Perhaps one day the law will be amended to permit those who love themselves so much to marry themselves. The law usually bends with social opinion, and we certainly receive exhortations from all kinds of self-development people to "love yourself." The marriage license, after all, is not the same as the marriage. We all know that a marriage is something created between two people. It is formed and reformed constantly through the experience of relating to another. It is a social work of art, and all of us are social artists in one way or another. As a result, every marriage is unique and has nuances and qualities suited only to the two parties shaping it. The marriage license only testifies to the existence of a marriage. It is a piece of paper that signifies an agreement between two people to spend their lives forming a marriage appropriate for their particular development and intentions. The license is not the marriage, but it is a physical sign that one is being formed. The marriage itself is invisible. It exists only so long as it is being created.

All agreements and contracts are similar in essence. Sometimes an attorney will whip out a template for an agreement, and both parties sign it. Is the agreement the piece of paper? How many partnerships do we know that have only the crudest papers to support them, and yet they last a lifetime? How many partnerships do we know that have reams of legalese to spell out every detail of their arrangement, but barely make it through the calendar year? It is sage advice to avoid a partnership with someone unless you have complete trust. Even a slight reluctance should be enough to give you pause. Like marriages, partnerships, agreements, and contracts are only as good as the social trust behind them, invisible to all except the hearts of those involved.

Where do agreements actually exist? Where is the reality of a marriage, an agreement, or a contract? Apparently somewhere between the parties. It isn't in one of the parties, nor is it in the other. It must be between them. But what is between them? I never saw a marriage in the air—up in the air, perhaps, but not in the air. To discover the reality of an agreement such as marriage, we need to shift our consciousness away from physical reality and into an invisible reality that lies between the parties. It is something neither possesses, yet both create.

Like music, it shifts and changes, wafts and eddies, and never endures beyond the moments it is created. Our consciousness has to leave this world and enter a world of soul space, wherein all human agreements thrive or die. Our feelings and thoughts live in this element of our souls. I am not using the term in a religious sense, but out of our everyday experience of some inner, usually subjective dimension that can expand to include another party for agreements and contracts. This is the place where transactions live their reality. It takes two parties to carry out a transaction. Nobody I know can sell something that no other party wants to buy. Buying and selling are two counterparts to an activity that starts in the physical world and ends up in the soul space between the parties.

The dance between the parties is easily perceivable and audible and can be recorded. The moment that this transaction is actually formed is instantaneous and between the two. It's the moment when both parties know that the transaction is realized. If one of the parties does not move in psychic terms, the other party cannot finish and achieve agreement. Imagine a purchase during which you believe a price has been set only to find out that other contingencies are expected. Perhaps no delivery is made without a large fee; the item does not include several parts; or the package did not indicate that no batteries are included. Until both parties know everything, the transaction is uncertain. Either party can still back down or out or continue the negotiations. Both parties are indispensable for a transaction. In the moment a transaction is consummated, both parties feel exaltation, relief, and a kind of joy that may even prompt them to reach out their hands to signal that they both realize what has happened.

In countries where bargaining reaches a high art, this moment of agreement can be pure joy. It does the soul good to reach agreement with another human being. If one party just pays what is asked for, the other party feels cheated—which they are, because they are cheated of the dance to culminate in a joyous transaction. Once I purchased a secondhand car, only a year old and still in warranty, from a reputable dealer, for $12,000 off the sticker price of a similar new car. I felt as though I had just saved myself $12,000. It was pure joy. I had forgotten that the dealer would not have sold it to me at that price unless it benefited him in some way that mattered.

Thus a transaction does not happen unless both parties feel they have gained or "won." Financial transactions are often win-win games, played millions of times a day. Cheating can occur, false pretenses are put forward, human nature being what it is, and some transactions are not in keeping with our civilized code of behavior. Still, such anomalies do not alter the essential character of the buying/selling transaction.

A financial transaction is a remarkable occurrence in which polarity generates movement and value. The healthy tension between the two parties engenders life and meaning. The polarity exists because two parties, each with their own needs, meet to satisfy their individual desires through the activity with the other party. They do not meet to create teamwork, nor do they have the same goal. They have individual goals and negotiate for the common ground called a transaction. Because each party wants something the other has, and because both parties are obliged to give something up that they have, a certain tension is created. The tension thus created between the two parties' needs has to be resolved to the satisfaction of both. Every such transaction stimulates the whole economy and provides meaningful work for many other people not directly involved in the transaction. The millions of transactions occurring around the globe are the keys to a healthy economy. This we all know and believe fervently. Our economy is our modern belief system externalized into transactional behaviors.

10. How Does Money Move?

B ECAUSE WE ARE accustomed to thinking of money as an object, we picture the movement of money as a flow of objects in a pipeline, so to speak. We imagine the force that moves money as a kind of pressure or physical push, just as we push other objects in the world. When we push a ball it moves. That's the way we picture the manner in which money moves. However, we are deluding ourselves. If I shovel all the money I have into a wheelbarrow and hitch myself to it for a ride around town I am certainly exerting a great deal of physical energy on the wheelbarrow and the money. I can take it down one street, back up another and around the square and through all the familiar and unfamiliar streets in my town. I will be exhausted from all the energy I have applied to this physical exercise, but, as far as money is concerned and as far as the economy is concerned, nothing has really happened. That is the remarkable thing. When we speak about the movement of money, we do not mean a physical movement at all. Money is, in fact, not susceptible to physical forces. Currency can be shoveled around the way any object can be shoveled around, but this kind of physical treatment of money as an object has no meaning.

Money moves only through what we call a transaction. Objects can be stolen and so can money as an object. A theft, however, does not show up in the economy. Some companies estimate or deduce an amount for theft or loss in order to write it off. It is a purely fictional number, accepted in accounting practice and permitted by law as an appropriate way to account for what we perceive as objects missing from our inventory and for which we have no other reasonable explanation. If the whole economy were filled with such events, there would be no movement of money at all.

Writing off a missing object is in itself a fascinating occurrence. The object has vanished from our inventory, and we are unable to account for its disappearance. Nevertheless, it once existed, so it must be somewhere in the world. Consequently, our tidy minds have to create a bookkeeping entry that accounts for it in our financial records. The object has now been accounted for in our records as no longer owned by the entity for which the accounts exist, even though we do not know where it is. We know for sure that objects don't just evaporate, as our belief in them is absolute. Therefore they must be somewhere at all times until they are consumed. As far as our economic records are concerned, such objects that have been lost or stolen are presumed to have been consumed. It is interesting to consider how "things" leave reality and enter the quasi-real world of accounts and books.

Money moves only when two parties reach an agreement and act on that agreement in such a way that an exchange between the two parties verifies and consummates what has been agreed. What occurs is a kind of handshake. Money moves when there is a significant, consciously intended "handshake." That's what a transaction is. It is the psychic counterpart of the handshake or agreement, and it lives actively in our souls to move money in a stream of value throughout our social life.

11. Economic Value

Value of an Object

In our story of the desk, John has no idea of the real value of the desk. Like most of us, John would prefer to have an expert opinion on its value. An expert could go down a checklist of criteria and eventually determine at least the range of values for the desk. In his heart, John knows that such an expert opinion would leave him dissatisfied. He simply wants the desk. Embodied in the desk are his experiences, images of his youth, echoes of his first experiences with books and writing, and the glow of early achievement. The desk represents a part of his youth that he treasures. The administrator also has no idea what the desk is worth. She knows that it has value for largely sentimental rather than utilitarian reasons, although its utility does matter. It is embedded in a whole community of people, its culture, and traditions at the Waldorf school. The very idea of selling it, especially to a stranger, is abhorrent to her. There is no objective, reliable basis for determining the value of any object, whether a desk, a garden tractor, bananas, or aspirin. The value of any object is revealed only through a transaction—buying and selling. The moment the seller agrees to a price that the buyer is willing to pay, the value lights up and is established.

As we saw in "John's Bargain," the moment the transaction is completed and the buyer leaves with the object of his choice, its value is concealed again. Is the desk really worth $750? Well, John doesn't know anymore, because there is no objective way to determine the value at this point. It was worth $750 in the moment of the sale. Which raises the question: What is value, and where is it? In a typical textbook on economics, you will read that value is stored in the objects. Every object, whether a teacup, a candlestick, or a banana, is deemed to have a value. Value, however, is not objective in the first place. An object has a value only in connection to someone, not in the abstract.

Could it also be true that value does not exist until two parties create it? One party must desire something enough to purchase it with personal resources from another party. However, the seller must also be willing to grant a value to the money used for the exchange. In a purchase, the value of the object and the value of the money used to purchase it are both created. In fact, the value of both is revealed simultaneously as a single value created by the exchange. Value is not stored in objects at all. It is created only in a financial transaction between two parties furthering their aims and intentions in life. Money moves when two parties engage in a transaction involving the creation of a value. The transaction by two parties actually establishes economic value in our social life. This mysterious element called value appears between the two parties, not in the individuals or in the objects. In the non-space between them, in the non-physical dimension between human souls, economic values arise and disappear like lights in the night; fireflies revealing the presence of the ethereal human creation we call economic value.

Values do not remain in human consciousness, nor do they remain in objects. Values are as transitory as human feelings, yet they are not entirely subjective, since two parties agree on a given value that describes both objects in a transaction. Of course, immediately after the transaction has been completed, the value so created is gone from consciousness and out of the interaction. It may happen that one party will begin to question the value they created or feel unfairly influenced by the psychological pressures of the other, or that they were not told the entire truth about the objects involved in the transaction.

Imagine an elderly person in need of more income being persuaded to purchase a hundred shares of a common stock, with assurances that the dividends have been at eight percent for several years in a row and will no doubt continue that way for years to come. Now we all know that there is always risk, and if risk is not fully disclosed, a purchaser might well overlook the risk for the sake of a steady income assured but not promised. After buying the common stock, it is too late to change one's mind, and the elderly person is very likely to learn the volatile nature of income risk, which is entirely in the hands of the issuer's management. Thus the value is good only for the moment of transaction, and any assurances of other values is entirely dependent on the people managing the organization.

Regardless of the complexities of any such transaction, the truth remains that a single value is created through the exchange and that the value does not adhere to the objects involved, does not endure, but melts away along with all the thoughts and feelings that emerged through the interaction. The ramifications of this important insight are explored in detail in section six.

VALUE OF CURRENCY

We acknowledge that one of the objects involved in the transaction, whether a sofa or an orange, immediately begins to be consumed or to deteriorate. The other object in the transaction, the currency, has a printed value and pretends to be immortal, even though its ability to act as a constant in any transaction is actually eroded or enhanced by inflation and other national and world economic and social processes. In other words, the pretended value printed on money is not a constant, but a variable. What matters is not the printed value on currency or the arithmetic value in calculations, but how it holds up in actual transactions.

Nations, through their monetary policies, do all they can to maintain a kind of pretend immutability for their national money in a world of constant mutability. If you happened to live in Germany in 1938, the pretence of immutable currency would have provided you a painful experience. At that time, you might pocket all the currency you owned, perhaps as much as 590 trillion deutsche marks, rush to the nearest grocery store to find it was not enough to buy a loaf of bread. All those trillions of deutsche marks were worth less than a loaf of bread. So, what is the value of any currency at any given time? The value is determined only by what it can purchase. Currency is no different from any other object, in that its value is unknown until a purchase is attempted. The transaction will reveal the value of the currency, just as the transaction will reveal the value of the purchased object. Put more clearly, every transaction creates one value shared by two objects being desired by the participating parties.

Most objects manufactured or created are the physical outcomes of human creativity and skill applied to the natural world. The human creativity and skill is employed to create objects or provide services, which can fuel human desires and be used in economic transactions. All that we produce are simply our desires and wishes externalized in society. Money enters every transaction, representing the ability of humans to create economic value. Money stands for our interactive creativity. It is a barometer of our social health and has as its main function to heal our social ills and support the further evolution of human beings. Which of our many desires is really worthy of our highest ideals? How many of us think before we buy, whether this transaction advances our development or retards it? When we make a purchase or sell an object, do we always consider the possible impact on our social life together?

Economic value is a social phenomenon; it does not endure, but must be created anew in each transaction. Much human energy has gone into creating the illusion that it continues to exist as a constant in our social life. The only reason the illusion can persist is that we continue to create it, depend on it, and believe in it. It is one of our most cherished beliefs, the most widely held religion of our time. We human beings, between one another in a non-physical dimension I call *soul,* create the whole economic life of our civilization. It is probably the greatest single illusion ever created by us. No movie, play, or book offers a challenge to the fiction of our economic system. *Star Wars* doesn't compare to it.

Imagine the more than two trillion dollars given for charitable purposes each year by foundations, corporations, families, and individuals in the U.S. Can you also imagine how much capital it takes to earn more than two trillion dollars in order to give it away for a good cause? Let us say, for the purpose of estimating at five percent growth, that we would need to invest about $40 trillion US dollars to make that much money. Do we know how those forty trillion dollars are invested? Do we know whether the forty trillion dollars is doing any good in the economy and whether it supports any enduring human values? For all we know, the more than two trillion dollars of good done by philanthropies is outweighed by what the forty trillion does in relation to the environment, poverty, human health, and well being.

When I say the economic life of civilization is an illusion, I use the specific word *illusion* because I do not believe it is a fantasy. We make this illusion real in our social life. It is an imagination that grows out of our soul life; we make it real through the power of our belief and the energy with which we arrange our lives around it. In fact, we create it repeatedly through our transactions, millions of times in a second around the globe, and we barely understand what we are doing. We do not fully understand what we are doing because, to understand it fully, we need to switch from physical perception to social or psychic perception, the realm in which all agreements and other psychic constructions exist. In other words, we need to perceive such realities with organs other than our physical senses.

We will take up that issue in section six later. We can grasp the true nature of money only by acknowledging the existence of the human soul where all economic value has its cause. Many of us may still perceive only some of the negativity and abuses in our present economic environment, but there is also the potential for much good. With our imaginative cognition we can comprehend money, identify the cause of its movement, and instill it with healing forces.

12. When Currency Becomes Money

CURRENCY IS AN object, but is not necessarily money. That's why we have two separate words. Let's imagine that we are marooned on an island with lots of necessary things such as food, clothing, utensils, and tools. We also have a bundle of U.S. bills with various amounts printed on them and amounting to $10,000. These bills may be useful for starting a fire or blowing one's nose, but they will not be useful as money. In fact, as long as we are marooned and alone on the island, our currency is not money. If another person, say, a man, becomes marooned on the island, he may have other items rescued from his vessel, but may lack food or certain tools. Barter then becomes possible with two people, but because the currency is useless, it is unlikely to be bartered. If suddenly a whole boatload of people arrive on the island, also shipwrecked, there is a possibility that our currency might become money. It isn't a sure thing, though. The people who arrive might have a different currency and not recognize your currency as having any use to them. What turns the object currency into money is the agreement among a community of people that it is money and can be used in transactions. Such a social agreement creates the possibility of any object becoming money. However, it still is not money until an actual transaction turns the currency into money.

I can take some pieces of paper, draw nice pictures on them, and print dollar signs and amounts on them. This is currency and can be offered to others to facilitate a transaction. In a sense, it is a kind of promissory note issued by a single person without the actual promise being spelled out. It is an assumed promise to replace the paper with a similar object if asked, to be honored by whoever's name appears on the paper. The fact that no person accepts it in a transaction is sad for you, but doesn't change the fact that it is currency. However, it is not money. Some person has to accept it in a transaction for it to become money. When people in a community tacitly or by common consent agree that the currency is money and use it to facilitate their financial transactions, only then does the currency become money and demonstrate its validity through movement. When it moves it is money, because it is alive within the circulation of value around the globe. When it rests in a safe place, it loses its identity as money. You may have a wad of bills in your mattress for safekeeping. While it is there its value is unknown. Whatever is printed on the currency is very likely an illusion, and it is certainly unverifiable until removed from the mattress and offered in a transaction. Money is not the object; it is the agreement and the movement.

In the process of describing this development of money, we have transported ourselves from the material world of sense-perceptible objects into the human soul world where commonly shared understandings and agreements live. Currency can be used by anyone, even when it quietly slips into movement under agreement as money. Money can be understood fully only as movement apprehended and created by two souls in agreement. It is then no longer the property of a single soul, but lives in the soul space between many humans. As long as you and I believe something is money, and as long as it works in an attempted transaction and supports our belief in it, that currency becomes money. It can be money only when it acts like money and facilitates an actual transaction.

Today human beings are anchored solidly in the material world. We barely notice that most of our cherished life activities dip in and out between physical experiences and soul experiences. If we want to understand money as it truly functions in our life, we must acknowledge the existence and presence of the soul. Our soul life sustains our belief system and enables an object to become money.

13. Our Soul Life and Economic Value

THE ONLY RELATIVE stability obtained in our soul life is won through our ability to think and to will, two powerful forces active in the human soul. Through thinking, the soul attempts to understand what is going on in one's life. Through the forces of will, the soul attempts to transform what is given in life to reflect one's intentions. To construct a table, for example, we first employ our ability to think so that we understand the use of various tools, how different kinds of wood respond to treatment, and how we visualize the potential product of our labor. We wouldn't even attempt to understand all of that without some will and a great deal of thinking. Understanding how to do things is not the same as doing them. Actually making the table requires the forces of will in our being, which we focus in a particular way to coordinate and direct our actions. Some determination and persistence is required. We employ some thinking in this process and a great deal of directed will.

A person's will may not always be productive or beneficial to humankind. The soul employs thinking, and the will determines how beneficial or productive our actions will be. We may be hindered by conditions of ill health or moral turpitude, which may lead to actions that are not beneficial. All manner of conditions can affect our ability to focus and coordinate the forces of will that live in us. The chief purpose of education and early childhood is to connect us through our souls to master the inner forces of will and engender a desire to be of service to others.

One way to understand thinking and willing is through the example of marriage. A marriage between two people cannot be based purely on feelings of love and affection. Marriage is deeply felt, but in addition it is associated with many concepts and pictures conjured up in us through thinking and willing. A marriage contains not only love, but also ideas and intentions. It is created jointly as a social act in a non-physical space between two people. Marriage has to be maintained, nurtured, and kept alive in the stream of time and the life lived together. In other words, marriage is not a license but a soul work of art, created by two people in a non-physical space enacted in a life of mingled souls. That soul space has to be objective so that both individuals can work on it. It also has to be illusive and tentative so that both may contribute to its life.

Similarly, economic values do not live in the physical world, nor are they expressed purely in the monetary calculations and instruments we use as shorthand to represent what we cannot perceive with our senses. Economic values are continually in flux, created anew with each transaction, only to evaporate an instant later, as discussed previously. A single new piece of information can alter the value we believe to be inherent in a painting, for example. What we believe its value to be changes dramatically if, for instance, we discover it was painted by the master's student and not the master. This applies equally to all objects. Any object will change its value in our eyes depending on what we know about it and believe its qualities to be, which usually cannot be seen with physical eyes. Our inner eyes of the soul perceive knowledge, wisdom, and qualitative attributes such as beauty, goodness, beneficence, and deliciousness. What we take into any transaction is the whole content of our soul life.

Altogether, created repeatedly all over our world, the evanescent economic values present the mirage of our economic system, which mirrors the soul conditions of humankind at any time or place. Consider how important and valuable a few drops of water become in the Sahara Desert. The possession of several skins of fresh water would make someone seem relatively wealthy. A bag filled with currency may not be as attractive in such a situation. Economic values must be variable, effervescent, and malleable to be of service to the evolving human being. They are our creation and, therefore, exist simply to serve us. They are objective only in the sense that all of us participate in upholding and shaping them.

These revelations about the connections between soul life and economic life are contained in the simple story of the man who desires a desk and the woman who desires money for her school. Between them they create an economic value that satisfies both desires and thereby adds another spark to the world's economic life. In fact, psychologists should be studying the movement of money to understand the inner life of humanity, and economists should be studying the soul life of humanity to comprehend the world circulatory movement of money, as the two appear to be inextricably linked. The soul life is the underlying reality for the impressive mirage of our economic system.

Money is healthiest when it moves rapidly throughout the world. It reveals a positive inner attitude in the souls of humans. When the movement of money slows or even approaches a standstill we are in grave danger, and all of us bring this about owing to our lack of confidence, optimism, and productive energy. The movement of money, its speed, and its quantitative fullness is a direct result of the general soul disposition of humankind.

14. What We Have Learned

WHAT HAVE WE learned so far from the story of "John's Bargain"? We discovered that the transaction we know as buying/selling tends to focus us on objects, and in doing so draws us into the material world. Transactions incarnate us into the world and accompany our appetites, desires, and seeming need for all kinds of material objects. Human desire is the motivating force that makes buying/selling possible. Whole industries, advertising, and the media have grown up around the potential for manipulating our desires to serve their ends. Such industries believe that most of us rarely think, that we are easily manipulated by the power of suggestion, are consumed by desires for anything and everything, and that we as individuals are solely responsible for what we purchase. Their responsibility is not for our welfare, as that is our business to determine—and rightly so. So long as we do not grow up and become responsible adults, we will always be manipulated easily.

We also know that the meaning of money is not in its nature as an object, but in its movement. Wealth could be redefined as the capacity to engage in transactions, move money, and participate in creating economic values. Some people have a lot of such capacity; others have less. All have some.

We also know that none of us is capable of moving money alone. All such physical movements of money that we do, like transporting currency around in our pocket, are pointless and meaningless. We need another party to engage with us in creating value, or it never appears except as a fiction, an illusion. The creation of real value requires two willing parties to engage, for example, in a buying/selling transaction.

We know that the movement of money is not a physical act, but a social act, one that plays out in the non-physical, psychic/social space between human beings. Currency appears as a physical object, but also serves as a social vehicle. Value appears nowhere in the natural world or even in the physical world, but only in the interactive, social space between human beings. Currency becomes money only when it serves a specific transaction, like buying a desk. In a specific transaction, currency leaves its nature as an object and becomes movement in the economic flow of value sustaining human social life. To understand our monetary transactions, we are taken right out of our physical, sensorial world and into the psychic world, where all the invisible activities such as love, growth, life, and progress live. We enter a realm of existence from which we derive the capacity—not yet fully developed—to shape and create our social future, not just because we idealistically hope for it or desire it, but because we will it out of our emerging higher nature.

We may pay a little more for an organic product because we know that it contains increased nourishment and benefits the farmers who strive to make the world's agriculture less dependent on artificial fertilizer and insecticides. By doing so, our transaction has a positive effect on the way the world is shaping up. When we purchase something simply because it is cheaper, even at the expense of our environment and the future conditions of the Earth, we reap a short-term financial benefit but we may also weaken our physical health and burden future generations with a dying Earth.

Economic values do not exist in the physical world, nor does money exist in the physical world. Rather, it exists as a kind of membrane between the physical world and the soul world. It is both an object, as currency, and an agreement; it lives one moment in physicality and the next in a soul element. Why? Because money comes alive when it moves through transactions and encourages human souls to mature and become responsible through their manifold transactions. Maturity is acknowledging all that lives in our souls and refining our inner life so that we become capable of healing our social life through monetary transactions.

Some economists insist that economic values are lodged in every object precisely because they do not want to acknowledge the soul as a reality and that it plays a distinct role in human economic activity. They have not developed the flexibility in their own souls to alternate between the visible and the invisible, between material existence and soul existence. Individuals are beginning to grasp this elusive truth, yet that is exactly what we have to do before we can comprehend the flow of economic value that sustains human economic activity: the movement of economic value, which is represented by currencies in modern cultures.

In trying to grasp the essence of money and economic value for which it is a surrogate, we have stumbled into the soul world and now realize that our economic system as a whole is a construct of our soul life. It continues to exist solely because we want it to and faithfully believe in it. First, we discover that money is not a physical object, nor is it susceptible to physical force. Second, we find out that money moves only in a transaction between two parties fulfilling their desires. Third, we realize that every transaction creates economic value, which is part of a worldwide belief system based on the creativity and productivity of human beings. Fourth, we have uncovered that we need to consider the soul life of individuals and groups if we wish to create a future state of economy that serves our highest intentions.

Imagine developing sense organs able to perceive our physical world simultaneously with the soul world. We would be able to perceive a rapidly ebbing and flowing of human feelings, thoughts, and impulses. Around every transaction that occurs in the world there would be the kaleidoscope of desires, joys, anticipation, disappointments, triumphs, and satisfactions. These are not visible, nor do they belong to the visible world we perceive with our normal senses. They are nevertheless present. Actually, it is precisely the world of myriad desires, intensifying and then fading, that really fuels the buying/selling transaction. Other transactions are different, but buying/selling is possible only because we have powerful desires that propel us into the dance around objects, services, and money. Let us continue our explorations with another story.

SECTION THREE

BORROWING AND LENDING

15. Janet's Emancipation

J ANET IS EMBOLDENED by what she considers extravagance on John's part and asks him to accompany her to the nearby department store. He comes along because he feels somewhat obligated to give in to one of her whims. After dinner they drive to a shopping mall. Janet meanders and slowly leads them into the department store, where she steers them toward the furniture section and they happen to stumble upon a sofa as if by accident.

"Oh, my!" she exclaims, "Have you ever seen anything so perfect?"

"Perfect?" asks John. "What kind of perfect?"

"I mean for our living room," Janet says. "We could finally get rid of that old sofa your parents gave us and begin to look a bit more presentable."

John promptly replies, "My parents' sofa was good enough for them and it's good enough for us. Look at how we use it all the time."

"Oh, John, just look at this one," she pleads. "This one doesn't have any spots, and just sit on it. It is so comfortable! When our child's nursery teacher comes to visit us next Thursday, I would feel much better with a sofa like this one in our living room."

"But I like the sofa we have now," responds John.

"Honey, let's put that one in the family room," continues Janet. "Wouldn't you like that?"

"This one looks a little fancy," says John. "And who knows how well it is made."

Janet quickly answers, "I don't know anything about that. I thought you should look at it and give me your expert opinion."

John insists on having the sofa turned up so that he can see the works. He examines the wood and metal parts, the various connectors. Then he looks at the webbing, the material and stitching.

"It seems well made." He says begrudgingly. "How much is it?"

"Only $648," says a man who appears suddenly, as if by magic, at their sides. He has been standing nearby unobserved and seems to be the sales person.

"$648!" John exclaims. "That's no bargain."

"Oh, it is," explains the sales person. He then goes into a long explanation of how it is made and how its construction is much better than your usual sofa, but because of this company's new manufacturing innovations, they are able to put it out for only $700."

John retorts, "I though you said it was only $648."

The man quietly answers, "For you it is, and just for today as part of the company's introductory offer. So you see it is a bargain after all."

"And it is much less than a desk," Janet interjects.

"Well, I'm sorry! We are not spending $648 on a sofa!" John says adamantly.

Then, from the look on John's face, Janet realizes it was a mistake to make any reference to John's purchase of the desk. "John ..." Janet begins.

"No! Absolutely not!" says John very firmly. "We are not buying this sofa."

"Oh, but we are," says Janet surprisingly; she is normally quite diplomatic, with little inclination for confrontations.

"Let's not fight about this," John whispers, motioning toward the salesperson, whom he has suddenly noticed. He starts to feel as if the salesperson may be questioning his manhood.

Janet explains. "I will be baking thirty loaves of our own homemade bread every week and taking in two of the neighborhood children after school every day. I'll be paid for both of those projects, and in just six weeks I will have $648 saved and ready to spend on this very sofa."

"How do you know you can earn such money?" asks John.

Janet goes into a short explanation of how these ideas have begun to be a reality and, further, that various people have asked for the bread and that two neighbors need someone to take their children until they return home from their jobs.

John doesn't know what to say. Suddenly he has lost any authority he thought he had over the expenditure. "His" money is no longer involved in this transaction; suddenly, "her" money has appeared. He feels he has no jurisdiction over this new kind of money. "Their" money and "his" money were clearly something he controlled, but "her" money is a new experience in his life, and he feels helpless. John finds himself graciously agreeing with Janet that the sofa is worth getting. "But the old sofa goes in the family room," he says with all the firmness he can muster.

Janet works out the details of a time payment without any interest for seven weeks while she accumulates the entire price. She also arranges for delivery and makes a small down payment. All of this is done without John's participation, although he stands by with growing admiration for how Janet is handling the negotiations and details. When the salesperson explains that Janet has to take the floor model or wait another eight weeks for delivery, she skillfully asks for an additional discount as well as free delivery. The final value of the sofa is blurred somewhat by the values of free delivery, discounts, and delayed payment. Between the two of them, the salesperson and Janet create a value and money moves.

⊷⊨◎ ◎⊨⊷

In this story we see that a value is being created in the transaction between the two parties—Janet and the department store. The so-called value that was created arose in the negotiations between Janet and the store. Each party had desires to be satisfied. The back and forth between them slowly but surely eased the natural tension needed in any transaction, and it culminated in an agreement that generated the acceptable value. We also see how the attention of all the parties, especially that of the potential buyers, was focused on the sofa, and how their consciousness was drawn down from all other considerations into the material world, represented here by the sofa.

Another key feature of the buying/selling transaction is that, once all the details have been worked out and both parties agree to it, the transaction is instantaneous. The value appears in the consciousness of both parties and then objectively between them as an agreement. Although there was no traditional handshake, the understanding around price and terms was explicit and eventually written into an actual paper agreement.

There was a time when a handshake was enough. If one of us refused to honor the deal, it could cause a duel, a gunfight, and possibly death for one of the parties. At a time when no one shook hands in greeting but only to seal a deal, a handshake was taken seriously. We see that a distinguishing feature of the buying and selling transaction is that the entire matter takes place in a single moment, the moment in which both parties agree and physically or symbolically "shake hands." The buying and the selling occur simultaneously in the same moment. Up to this point, the characteristics of any buying/selling transaction are clearly discernible in this story. However, something a little different is also revealed here.

16. Defining the Participants

S OMETHING NEW EMERGES from the story of the sofa; it can be complicated to identify a party to a transaction. Such a transaction can be consummated only by someone having the legal right to do so. The law recognizes an individual, a legally established partnership, or incorporation, which can act as an individual. Only *individuality* is valid under the laws of our land. To conduct a binding transaction, the law requires a single party or a group organized to act as a single party.

If a few of us wander off the street into a store and want to purchase something with a signature, the store may get us all to sign individually, but generally the store will look for one of us to take the responsibility. Whoever signs is usually the legal party to the transaction. If for some reason we pool what we have in our pockets and pay cash, the store no longer cares about the finer points of ownership. The portion of the purchased item owned by each of us is left for us to determine among ourselves. The transaction is completed instantaneously; the value has been created. The receipt, however, if one is requested, is usually issued to only one party. If the item is returned to the store by another individual, the refund may be denied. Again, this question of a party's identity is not just the recognition of a body; it must be an established legal identity if any record or recourse is to be honored. When we buy a candy bar, we pay a few bills and disappear without a receipt. If we return with it half eaten and want our money back, it is entirely up to the owner of the store to determine whether the transaction occurred.

This question of the transactor's legal identity is crucial to further understanding money. It emerges so significantly out of our simple story that we need to pause here and investigate it more thoroughly. One aspect is clear; a legal party to a transaction, other than a cash transaction, must be an adult, which our law defines as anyone over the age of twenty-one. Someone at the age of eighteen may be considered almost an adult and therefore able to perform certain socially approved acts. In some states of the U.S., even someone at the age of sixteen is considered so close to being an adult that certain social activity is allowed, such as driving a vehicle. Another factor is the mental condition and health of the individual. The person must be considered of sound mind as determined by a licensed medical practitioner. Certain activities also require the physical health of a person to be verified by a physician.

The person's social class, gender, or profession no longer plays a leading role in determining a legal party to a transaction. This was not always so. There was a time in the human history when a woman was not considered mature enough to sign documents, or at least not without the supervision of a responsible male party. There was also a time when only persons of a certain class or level of social standing were considered appropriate to be party to a binding transaction. In fact, as we go back in history, we find a remarkable evolution of the human consciousness. Moreover, we find the slow emergence of what we take for granted today—the presence of individuality in the human being, separate from family, social alliances, and even professional or village identities. For example, the earliest names came from a type of trade. Smith was a wrought iron tradesperson, and the ancestors of someone named Weaver were obviously weavers. Still earlier the names came from the village, like Timothy of Glendale, or Arthur of Camelot. The fact that we still have second names to denote the family is important for identification, but there was a time when the family affiliation meant a great deal more than it does today. We are liberated in large measure from many of the restrictions of the past, which dictated what you could be and do, based on family or rank.

In section six, I will use a sequence of ancient myths and stories to describe symbolically how individuality in human nature evolved and slowly developed to its present prominence. These myths and semi-historic stories will illustrate that individuality, as we know it today, emerged only gradually in human evolution. The sequence of stories will demonstrate how human consciousness was initially child-like, existing in a protected world of parent-like entities we knew as "the gods." Those gods slowly withdrew from guiding humans; leaving more and more space for human beings to make their own decisions. This sequence of stories will show the evolutionary process of the law and how it came to exist as we know it today. We will also see how, as human beings, we could not have matured sufficiently to recognize our individuality, except in an environment from which the gods gradually retreated to teach us and permit us to develop.

Today, every person over the age of sixteen strives to be recognized as an individual, separate from family and other affiliations. *Our highest ideal is to be individuals, free to think and act within the context of a community. We all aspire to that wonderful, very modern condition.* Without the evolutionary process of consciousness, we would not be the individuals we are today. We could not have generated the concept of law, and we could not have evolved the nature of money to the point where it has become our instrument for establishing social health in our time. Nor could we have fulfilled our inherent potential to inherit the future of our race and the world in which we were allowed to incubate.

Now let us consider the other two financial transactions in order to discover some of their distinguishing features and what they reveal about human nature and human social life.

17. SURPRISE!

JANET AND JOHN had completed the purchase of the sofa and were fulfilling all the conditions of the sale. Janet went to work baking loaves of bread and started a small babysitting venture twice a week in her home. Both projects were going well and, owing to her industry, she began to be known around the neighborhood. People bought the bread, and they started sending their children to her, while asking for additional time for their children—three times a week and some even clamoring for five times a week.

Both she and John were amazed as the demand grew and their bank account seemed to swell. John tried to be as helpful as possible and became more involved, sometimes returning children to their homes when the parents were delayed or helping to straighten out their living room after the children left.

One evening, after a particularly hard day, John suggested they go out for dinner and splurge in celebration of their success. Janet rose to the occasion, dressed up, and together they drove to a well-known restaurant in a shopping mall—the one, coincidentally, where they had purchased the sofa.

During the meal a man, seated alone and having a large salad, kept looking over to where they sat. With a slight smile on his face, he sometimes held Janet's gaze for quite a long time. Janet looked away, but after awhile noticed he was again staring across to their table. Knowing what a strong temper John often had, she did not mention it to him. She wasn't quite sure, but could it be that the strange man was flirting? He did look somewhat familiar but she could not place him.

They enjoyed their meal and, as they often did these days, began talking about their growing business project, whether to expand it, and if so, how. They ordered desert and coffee, and suddenly the stranger from the nearby table was standing at their table smiling at them.

"Hello," he said. "Remember me?"

John and Janet both stared at him puzzled. "Well," Janet finally stammered, "you do seem a bit familiar."

"The sofa—the one you bought from my department store." The man explained. "I was the salesperson who made the arrangements for you to purchase it."

"Oh," exclaimed Janet, "of course, now I remember you. How do you do?"

"I am fine! How are you? Are you enjoying the sofa?"

"Yes, very much," answered Janet.

"There is something I would like to ask you. May I sit down?"

Janet and John looked at each other, but out of politeness did not object when he took an empty chair at their table.

The man looked at them for a moment and then hesitated before he spoke. "When the two of you came into the store to look at that sofa, I had no particular reaction. You were potential customers and, of course, I was interested in you, but thought nothing further about our meeting. However, as we were dealing with each other over the sofa, I gained more and more respect for the both of you and how you handled the purchase. I was very impressed with your plan, Ma'am, of starting to bake special bread and take care of neighborhood children in order to raise the money needed to buy the sofa. How is that going, by the way?"

"Very well," Janet said. "If you are worried about us paying for the sofa, you needn't. We have already done that and are putting some away and even making more, we are so successful."

"That's great," the man said. "I was sure that you would. From my experience of you, I have concluded that you are both special people with lots of capacity, brains, and willingness to work hard. I am sure you are and will continue to be successful. I felt I was meeting a fellow entrepreneur. That's why I wanted to talk with you about my idea."

"Your idea?" Janet asked.

"Yes. For many years now I have been working out a small software program for automatic internal routing of emails through a network. It is remarkably simple to install and provides extremely useful service to any organization that operates a server. I don't want to talk too much about it, because as you can imagine, I need to keep secret many of the details. I have obtained a patent and within the next month I plan to start presenting it to various firms for production and distribution rights. I expect it to be snapped up." He paused.

"That's wonderful. I'm glad for you. I hope you will be very successful." Janet commented.

"The problem is that I have done all the work and everything I could without involving any outside investors. However, in order to do the marketing, the presentations, and the negotiations around agreements, I will have to spend money for the first time. I have saved about $15,000, which I am willing and prepared to spend on this idea, but it's not enough. I wonder if you might be in the position to lend me about $7,000. I expect to sign a promissory note and will promise to repay the amount in full with interest within a ten-month period. What do you think?"

John and Janet were astonished. It took them completely by surprise. Actually they were shocked! They associated the man with the buying of the sofa and viewed him as a salesperson. His request to borrow money seemed out of keeping with their relationship to him. It just didn't go together. They felt annoyed that he would dare to ask them.

"Why don't you go to a bank?" John asked.

"I don't think a bank would consider a loan like this. It really requires venture capital, but if I go that route I will probably end up losing control of the product. Those guys play hardball and have no interest in anything except to make money—lots of it! I may have to do that, but I am hoping I can find some sympathetic folks like you who will see the potential in this product and give me a hand."

"If a bank will not do it, does it make sense for us to do it?" John asked with just a touch of belligerence in his voice, "even if we had the money."

"What would make you feel safer?" the man asked.

"Are you married?" asked Janet. "Where do you live? Do you have children? What kind of a house do you live in? How long have you had the job in the department store? Do you have any other debts?" Janet caught herself, realizing the questions were tumbling out without getting any answers.

That started the conversation and it continued for another hour. They ordered more coffee and Janet pulled out a small pad and pencil from her purse and started to take notes. After they exhausted all their questions, Janet said they needed to think about his request and they agreed to phone each other, but the man urged that they have another face-to-face meeting.

Eventually, after obtaining some collateral and a meeting with the man's wife in his home, Janet and John made the loan with some misgivings, but also a feeling they were helping a responsible person make his good idea into reality. They knew they had no business making such a loan, but they made it anyway out of feelings of being involved too deeply to get out of it. They began to have some confidence in this energetic man and began to feel that he actually meant to achieve what he set out to do. He was very businesslike in how he set up the loan, with a promissory note and a letter of agreement that spelled out the terms. He even put up collateral in the form of his house, which still had a mortgage on it but also plenty of equity.

So ends this part of the story. I will describe the third part of this story in chapter 22.

How very different this transaction is from the transaction involving the purchase of the desk or the sofa. Let's assemble our observations and look at each of the main characters, what their conduct reveals, and what this story adds to our understanding of money.

First, notice the gist of the questions Janet asked the man. Initially, his name was not known, but in the course of time, once the agreements were established, it was of course disclosed. The name of the salesperson was not important to purchasing the sofa. The only important subject was the sofa and how to obtain it. All of Janet's questions prodded at the identity and nature of the man asking for a loan. Janet felt she had to learn all she could about him even to consider such a loan. She wanted to know about his assets, how he lived, and whether he was alone or had a family. How secure was his job, and was he generally inclined to repay loans? Did he own a car and how had he paid for it? If he had a car loan, she would want to know whether he had repaid that loan on time and in full. Clearly, when it came to lending someone money, the purpose of the loan was useful information, but more important was the character and context of the borrower, thus Janet wanted to know everything she could about him.

Why did she need to know so much? There is something about the nature of this transaction, lending/borrowing, which depends more on the nature of the individuals involved than a purchasing transaction does. After making her purchase, Janet barely remembered the salesperson. He simply was not the focus of her attention. In a loan situation, however, the focus is on the borrower. The lender cannot seem to make a decision on whether to lend or not without delving into the nature of the borrower. The lender feels his or her part of the transaction is vulnerable, and this cannot be eased without knowing the person borrowing. The necessary knowledge has to be factual, not subjective. Liking the borrower helps, but is not as important as establishing an objective basis for trust. The loan agreement, the promissory note and its terms, form the basis of confidence in the ability of the borrower to carry the debt and to repay it. Promises are wonderful but soon forgotten in the rush of time and life's events. Something more tangible than a promise is needed. The potential lender uses an objective route to probe more deeply into the psyche of the borrower. The lender is trying to uncover something in the biography and life circumstances of the borrower that will provide enough confidence to lend and to find a connection that supports trust.

By asking personal questions, perhaps both the lender and borrower are dimly aware that the transaction has all kinds of karmic implications. It's as though the transaction itself automatically binds them into a relationship that has serious consequences beyond the financial ones. What if Janet decides not to lend the money; how will that affect their developing relationship? Will lending the money bind her in a relationship that she may not want? Moreover, what if the man defaults on the loan? What will that do to their relationship? Will it make them enemies, whereas a friendship now exists as a possibility? All these potential karmic implications are not mentioned, but they are present in the background of their discussions.

18. LENDING CREATES KARMA

IN THE CASE of a bank loan, some vulnerability (the personal or karmic implications) is masked by an objective assessment that determines whether the borrower has enough assets, which the bank can seize in the event of default. However, no bank wants to seize assets as a routine means to recover loans. The collateral a bank seeks is simply a necessary part of the transaction. In the final analysis, the bank must still gamble on the character of the borrower. The bank obtains credit information and leans heavily on the borrower's record—behavior with other lenders and whether other promises have been fulfilled with lenders. The bank assumes that, if other loans and credit card balances have been paid faithfully, the prospective borrower is more likely to repay this loan. One popular joke suggests that banks lend money only to those who can prove they don't need it. The emphasis on having sufficient assets that can be seized supports that concept. Banks do not generally exist to help destitute people with good ideas. Their purpose is to advance the activities of those who have already demonstrated the ability to succeed and who have a track record strewn with profits and implemented strategies of financial gain. They will also tend to lend anyone enough funds to acquire an asset worth more than the amount of the loan.

Are all banks alike? Of course not. There are wonderful banking activities going on around the world. Some banks are involved in "micro lending," while others have unique approaches to help emerging entrepreneurs become credit worthy. There are also socially constructive banking operations and investment firms. We live in a time when new, socially constructive actions are arising even in the staid halls of our banking establishments.

This little story makes it clear that, whereas purchasing tends to focus us on the material objects and to foster the incarnating process by leading us into the material world, the borrowing /lending transaction has a different character. It leads people into relationships with one another.

Borrowing/lending builds karma, because it leads us to involvement in one another's biographies, life goals, and purposes. The term *karma* here does not refer to something mystical or strange. It means simply that the transaction has long-term personal implications that either enhance the relationships between the parties or possibly destroy them or otherwise lead to negative future consequences. It is easy to see the short-term implications within the present lifetime of the parties to a loan. I myself prefer to consider the ramifications over a longer period of, say, several lifetimes. For me, karma is a little bit like a bank account, in which credits and debits are recorded and require various actions to restore a healthy balance. Borrowing/lending is a transaction that engages us as human beings in the community of humanity. It lures us out of our independent individuality to recognize our interconnectedness. The attention is on our humanity and on our relationships.

Why would Janet get so involved with the salesperson? At first she couldn't even remember his name. Why does John seem to have a more distant connection with this transaction? Could it be that borrowing/lending is possible only on a personal level (excluding for the moment the somewhat unfeeling business of banks in general) and based on some past connection? Is it that some connectivity of past lives is playing into our present relationships and influences the economy through the borrowing/lending transaction? It is difficult to isolate and test this theory, because we are so unskilled in our reflections on past lives.

We might wait for a bus in a small crowd, stand next to a stranger, and start a tentative conversation. Why, because someone told us we ought to be friendly? Well, there are others standing around waiting for the bus. Why this person? Did we notice that we actually selected this person? It wasn't just because the person was the nearest or had a pleasant face; or was it? Perhaps to someone else, that face would not appear as pleasant. It is a mystery why we feel comfortable with certain people and not with others. None of the explanations of psychology are quite satisfying. When we review an actual experience of this sort, we usually find that something in us was attracted or drawn to something in the other person, and that we have a variety of feelings that facilitated a connection.

Karma is the balancing force in the universe that records our connections, weighs their impact on our soul development, and causes us to engineer new meetings and interactions, including those of lending and borrowing. Karma is not a physical force. It is an invisible cause whose effects we are sometimes sensitive enough to feel in what happens to us.

In the case of Janet and the salesperson, something plays into the transaction from another lifetime. It is highly unusual for anyone to consider a loan of that size under the specific circumstances of the story. There has to be a compelling force at work on Janet for her to consider this loan. Moreover, what gave the salesperson the idea that he could borrow money from her? How dare he ask? On what basis could he feel that he had even the slightest chance of success? Why did Janet even continue the conversation? It was out of place, and John tried unsuccessfully to point this out. Something in Janet, however, led her to ask questions that involved and lured her into the transaction.

She could easily have said, "I'm sorry we don't have the money, and I don't lend to strangers." That would have ended it. Even if the man had continued to ask, which he certainly would have done, she could be firm and refuse any involvement. It is almost as if from another lifetime, an inkling of what may have been their connection was playing into the conversation out of subconscious depths and coloring their movement toward this transaction.

We conclude that borrowing and lending not only involves us with one another and creates conscious interdependencies, but also rests on some familiarity rooted in the past. It takes a bit of nerve to ask someone for a loan. Most of us don't feel we can ask just anyone for a loan. It has to feel right. This feeling right has something to do with the nature of our past connection with a potential lender. Something in our soul enables us to ask what we otherwise feel to be an awkward question. Some connections are present from earlier in life; others exist at a deeper level and arise from a previous life.

Those who have no loans live a comparatively self-sufficient existence; those who are in debt to many lenders walk about with a feeling that their existence rests on the contributions of many others, thus furthering the development of their life stories. After all, when we lend money it usually furthers that person's intentions in life. True, sometimes it is to get them out of a tight spot, but we usually tend not to lend for such reasons. We feel a lot more comfortable lending to someone who has a plan, a purpose and vision to accomplish with the money.

Past karma opens the possibility of borrowing/lending because, through the transaction, future karma is knitted into our psychic fabric and makes its effects felt in future lives. Bank borrowing and credit card borrowing are somehow depersonalized. We think of such loans coming to us out of a vast anonymous pile of money. Nevertheless, the transaction itself still has this quality of personal and long-term karmic implications just by virtue of the nature of this transaction. After all, too many bad loans will cost any loan officer the job. Many very good loans, on the other hand, might lead to a promotion. The consequences of lending/borrowing are inescapable; they move us into the psychic climate, where we live as a community of human beings. Essentially, every loan, when structured properly, helps the borrower either regain a footing in life or accomplish a cherished objective. Because individuals are assisted in their life goals, every loan has deep social consequences. If that isn't karma building, I'd like to know what is.

19. THE VALUE OF A LOAN

WHAT IS THE value of the $7,000 Janet is lending? Is it simply the face value of $7,000? In fact, she does not know, at least yet. Of course, she will certainly find out. It may be worth nothing if the man does not repay it or if he procrastinates and eventually fails in his venture. Much of the loan's value depends on the character and capacities of the borrower. If he is industrious and clever and has some good luck, he may succeed in his project, through which he might gain the means to repay the loan with interest. Even if he succeeds with the project, however, he may still avoid repayment of the loan. Further, he may fail in his project and still repay the loan. Whether he repays depends largely on his character.

We do not know the nature of the element from a previous lifetime that plays a role in the transaction. Does Janet feel obligated to him because of something that involved them in a past lifetime? Does the salesperson have a feeling toward Janet, lingering in his soul, of "being owed something," based on what plays into the transaction from his side of a previous life occurrence? Perhaps he has a feeling of triumph that he was able to exact a material gain from Janet in this lifetime? Alternatively, does he feel he has an inner right to ask this of her, based on some ancient indebtedness? We cannot answer these questions, because we lack the capacity to view our past lives and our past connections to one another. However, we can be awake to this possibility especially at key turning points in our lives and when considering a loan.

Whenever we engage in borrowing/lending, we can become sensitive to a faint memory or a magical melody softly playing in the background, reminding us that we live now by the grace of earlier experiences and that, wherever we turn, the residue greets us. As long as we are simply buying/selling with one another, such questions do not arise. As soon as we engage in lending/borrowing, they are present, like the harmonies to a distant melody. They sweeten or bring discord into the transaction, but we are mostly only semiconscious of them. It takes an open mind and an awakened heart to be aware of them.

Put yourself into the shoes of a micro lender like the Grameen Bank, which provides funds to the very poorest of the poor in Bangladesh.1 Imagine after many discussions, lending $2,000 to a group of three women who bake nourishing bread for their community and need a larger, more industrial oven. Gradually, the bakery flourishes, the loan is repaid and a new application comes in for a loan of $5,000 to add a larger store space to one of the houses. Consider the trust that is built up between the parties. Think of the shared joy in success and the feelings of gratitude from both parties for how people are able to help one another accomplish valuable, productive work.

In Shakespeare's *Hamlet,* Polonius tells young Laertes, "Neither a borrower nor a lender be." Of course that would be his advice; he was an old man wrapping up his life experiences and packaging them to obtain greater peace of mind. The last thing he wanted would be more karmic involvement. That's for people who are in the throes of an active life. Elderly people avoid lending and borrowing. There are many reasons for this, but the most common is a feeling that there isn't enough time to play out the involvement with the life of a loan. In many cases there is also a sense that, in order to make a secure loan, an elderly person has to learn a great deal about the borrower and gain ever-deeper knowledge of the person's character, and with this greater knowledge of the other human being comes greater involvement. Elderly people usually don't want more involvement. It is all right to chat a bit and surf over the interesting bits of other people's lives, but it becomes scary for them to engage on the level necessary for a loan. For example, I very rarely have a serious conversation with my contemporaries. Mostly, they are content to stay on the surface, enjoy the tidbits of conversation, humor, and descriptions of restaurants, tours, cruises, and families. I can just imagine what would happen if I asked one of them to lend me money. In no time at all, my wife and I would be ostracized and looking for another place to live.

On the other hand whenever I visit a school or a college and meet with young folks, the conversation almost immediately gets into essentials. They are not content with chitchat. They want to know and understand what life is all about. They want to know how they can navigate life's remarkable shoals and how they can act with certainty and inner confidence in a world without very good signposts.

These examples show us that lending/borrowing is a transaction avoided by the elderly and is generally beyond the means of the young. It belongs particularly to midlife, when enough time remains to live out all the implications of the loan.

Of course, the value of a loan depends on the capacities and character of the borrower, and the lender remains vulnerable to the borrower throughout the life of the loan. That raises another matter of interest.

20. TIME AND LOANS

O NLY A PART of the loan transaction occurs immediately, while the remainder lingers on in perhaps monthly or quarterly increments. Eventually, in a year, three years, five years, even thirty years, the transaction is consummated. That's a remarkable difference from a purchase transaction, which is completed instantaneously. In the blink of an eye, the purchase transaction has occurred, agreed to by both parties, and done. The fact that the seller sweetens the deal with lay-away plans and time payments, with or without interest, is beside the point. Those are mixtures and hybrids of transactions in which the seller combines a selling/purchase transaction with a lending/borrow-ing transaction. To complete the sale, the seller couples it with a loan, packaging two different transactions into a single bundle. For now, we are investigating pure transactions to understand their essence more easily.

Any loan has time built into it. The promise includes a definite period, during which the borrower is expected to maintain conscious-ness of the obligation to the lender. A moment is designated, agreed upon, and promised, at which point the obligation is to be settled. Under the law, the borrower is then subject to legal actions to enforce the promise made under the agreement. Because people tend to remem-ber quite different versions of an event, it has been found expedient to write down all such terms and contingencies to be certain that an agreement has been secured, after which both parties sign the docu-ment. The document maintains that, regardless of how it is remem-bered, an objective testament has been formulated that both parties agree to be accurate and enforceable under the law of the land.

Each party experiences the time between the signing of the agree-ment and the fulfillment of its terms quite differently. The lender feels the weight of the passing time in uncertainty and may show signs of nervousness, even dropping by occasionally to see "how things are going." The borrower, on the other hand, is amazed at how quickly the time zips by. When the borrower signs the agreement, the term, whatever it may be, seems adequate. Now the time flies and the borrower must rush to accomplish everything planned for the borrowed money.

At the time of payback, both are likely to be relieved. Clearly, lending/borrowing is not a comfortable transaction that yields unmitigated joy and happiness. Along with the time, a tension builds because the transaction has not been completed. This tension gives the money employed in the loan a certain aura of slowness, as if dragging its feet.

A purchasing transaction is quick and behaves with alacrity. The preparatory dance may be quite long, but the actual transaction is spontaneous and speedy. In terms of the money involved, it has a complimentary quality. In the purchase transaction the movement of money is fast. In no time it has moved through the store to supply inventory and on to distributors, then to manufacturers, and all the time the banks are involved to make it move as quickly as possible. We might characterize the money involved in purchasing as young money, vigorous money, or, in our new terminology, young movement, vigorous movement, dancing, jumping, and running movement.

There is something a bit slower and more ponderous about the transaction involving a loan. Even though there is a given moment in which the basic terms of the loan have been agreed upon, the very nature of the agreement has time built into it. There is no way to make a loan without specifying time. If you do, woe to you; you deserve to reap the consequences. Money involved in a loan situation is more sedate, somewhat more middle-aged, a little tired, and even sickly. The movement lingers, is more measured, and lives life in a less lively way as it rests in the books as an accounts receivable or a liability. This is older money in a movement that has lost its vitality. It doesn't have a "real" life in the same way as money involved in a purchase. It lives a shadow existence in the accounts.

Perhaps that is why almost all lenders prefer some form of time payments. They give the lender some assurance that there is movement during the waiting period. We have greater confidence when money is in movement that the human intentions behind the agreement are taken seriously. We begin to believe the agreement is real.

What is really going on when we engage in financial transactions? We are discovering that it is not such an abstract activity as it first seemed. Let's summarize what we have learned. We have seen that money as movement acquires characteristics through the type of transaction that brings about its movement. A buying/selling transaction invigorates the movement of money. A borrowing/lending transaction restrains the movement of money. In general, we know that value is created through any transaction, but the value is determined by different factors in each transaction. In a buying/selling transaction the value is determined by what is exchanged. The value arises through the exchange. The sofa does not attract more value than does the money, nor does the money attract a greater value than the sofa. The actual transaction creates a value that is shared in common by both simultaneously. In a loan situation a value is also created, but not instantaneously. It is created over time and depends on the capacities and character of the borrower. The quality of the movement is also quite different. It lingers, coasts through time, and only gradually creates value.

21. EFFECTS ON THE WORLD

Now we need to factor in another observation to understand the difference between these two types of transactions, buying/selling and lending/borrowing. The purchasing/selling transaction draws us into the material world. However, it also allows people to have a direct influence on events in the material world. For example, in the past several decades, we have seen the growth of organic and biodynamic farming methods. Why is this? People have grown more conscious of health and how the quality of nutrition either engenders or hinders good health. Individuals demand more health-giving produce and products. Whenever such a product becomes available, it is purchased. Whenever an item is purchased it stimulates the whole world economy to produce more of the same item. Our purchasing power determines what farmers grow and what manufacturers produce.

This is a living example, and there are thousands of them, of how the buying/selling transaction is our device for bringing about powerful short-term changes on the face of the Earth. Another example can be seen in the chemicals individual people feel are safe to use in household cleaning. The sale of biodegradable soaps and alternative dishwashing as well as laundry detergents have climbed dramatically. Whatever we buy determines what is produced. As we become more conscious of our health and what hinders it, we buy items that may be quite scarce initially, but as our demand increases, producers gradually respond to meet our needs.

Buying/selling allows human beings to insert their social intentions, their deepest interests and yearnings, into space. Buying/selling transforms space. Borrowing/lending inserts our human relationships from present lives and past lives into time. It colors our sense of community and reasserts our various obligations, experiences, and feelings of who is aligned with our intentions. Through lending, we support our compatriots' social values. We don't affect space, but we do influence our contemporary human community through the transaction of borrowing/lending. Lending usually empowers someone to fulfill a purpose or a dream or to overcome a mistake or avoid the consequences of a bad decision. In any event borrowing/ lending plays into time and inserts into it the drama of our ongoing relationships.

The buying/selling transaction affects the world because it is fueled by human desires. We used to think that *need* stimulates buying/selling. This is still true, but we actually need very little, whereas we *desire* a great deal. If need stimulates ten percent of all buying/selling, desire stimulates something like ninety percent. Much can be learned about the human soul by studying buying/selling activity around the world, in different regions and under different social conditions.

In contrast to the buying/selling transaction, the lending/borrowing transaction always enables someone to accomplish something that would not have been possible without the help of another. The transaction is fundamentally an enabling force in our social life, demanding a joint effort. The transaction supports another's intentions and enables a person or organization to move forward and realize a plan.

The following chart provides a summary of where we are at this point.

FACTOR	PURCHASE	LOAN
VALUE DETERMINED BY:	exchanged components	human capacities and character
TRANSACTION SPEED:	instantaneous, quick	over time
CHARACTER:	youthful	middle-aged
HUMAN CONSEQUENCES:	incarnate into matter	draws us into relationships karmic repercussions
EFFECTS:	humanizes space	dramatizes time
MOTIVES:	to fulfill soul desires	to support another's intentions

To complete the trilogy of transaction types, we will study the third type of transaction. Many economics texts do not acknowledge the transaction of giving/receiving as a legitimate transaction that influences the economy. In recent years, however, as we have become more aware of the charitable element in our social life as a real strength, we have begun to focus more attention on it. I maintain that giving/receiving is a legitimate transaction that has a legitimate role to play in our everyday economy. Let's look at this third transaction type with another story that I call *Success!*

SECTION FOUR

GIVING AND RECEIVING

22. SUCCESS!

A FTER JANET AND John loaned the salesperson $7,000, they received monthly phone calls from him, explaining that all was well and that he was using most of his weekends meeting with prospective companies and stirring up quite a bit of interest. So far he had not worked out a leasing or sale agreement that made sense for him, but they were not to worry. He always thanked them again and reiterated his determination to be a success and repay them. At the end of ten months, they received a check for the full amount plus interest accrued. Janet was pleased and felt reaffirmed in her judgment of human nature. John was a little surprised, but happy to have the money back in their account where he thought it should have remained in the first place. Their own little business prospered in a small way, and when Janet was expecting their second child, John took a larger hand in both the baking and the after-school childcare.

When they visited the local public school, their first child was about ready for first grade. It was very large and they felt hustled about from one administrator to the next without getting to see what was actually going on in a classroom. When periods ended, the halls were crammed with children, none of whom looked very peaceful or happy, almost as though they were primed for some mischief they were not allowed to act out. When John and Janet finally met their child's prospective teacher, Janet took an instant dislike and became very stubborn. She decided she would not trust her precious child to such a shallow, uncultured person.

John and Janet talked about their concerns and John had a similar feeling, though he was not as adamant. He had never particularly liked school, and he argued that school was not for liking, but for suffering through. In his heart he worried a bit for his gentle, inquisitive child. Then he remembered the Waldorf school, but he couldn't remember where it was. John looked it up in the phone book, but it wasn't listed. He called information and searched under various area codes. Finally he told Janet about it and she seemed surprised, because she had seen an announcement in the local paper describing an open house at the Waldorf school. They looked through the last few days' newspapers and finally found it.

That afternoon, they visited the school. They were welcomed warmly and made to feel that they were important in the life of the school. They met the teacher, who was friendly and heartening. She took in their child, spoke kindly with him, and engaged him in some of the work they were doing in another class. That day, to their own complete astonishment, they enrolled him in the Waldorf school. They had never thought of sending their children to private schools, but somehow this seemed important for their son as well as for them.

That's how it happened that they became connected with the very Waldorf school from whom John had purchased his beloved desk. Over the years, as they became increasingly involved in the school, he told the story of his purchase many times, almost with a sense of wonder at how it all seemed to be choreographed. John thought such things happened only in stories, not in real life.

Eventually their second child was enrolled in the school, too. They became involved in an auction to raise funds for the school, and then Janet was asked to take charge of the school's holiday fair. She organized the parents to knit sweaters and make wooden toys, and asked for gifts in kind from local suppliers and generally made the fair a resounding success.

One day, she and John were called to participate in a meeting at the school to discuss the future of the school. The board of trustees unveiled a plan to add an auditorium to the modest school building they occupied. An architect was present, and he described his view of how the auditorium would look and how it would enable all the children and their parents to meet at assemblies, special events, and performances.

This event began a completely new chapter in Janet's life. She was asked to serve as the capital campaign chair, but after thinking about it, she turned it down, feeling that the campaign needed a big name at its head, someone well known in the community who respected and loved the school. The administrator approached Janet with another suggestion. A parent in an upper grade had built up a large software company and was independently wealthy. He had one child who had already graduated from the school and another in grade ten. Janet did not feel it was her job to interview potential campaign chairs and suggested that the administrator mention it to the board of trustees.

"They respect your judgment, and if you meet him, maybe you would agree with me that he is perfect for the job," the administrator responded. "Besides, he is in my office right now paying his tuition, and you could meet him informally."

"All right," said Janet. "I'll say hello."

The administrator led the way into her office. The man sat at a corner of her desk writing out a check and looked up.

"Hello, Janet," he said. "I thought we might meet again one day."

Janet couldn't believe her eyes. It was Mr. Jessup, the former salesperson, now a little older with some gray hair around the temples, well-dressed and exuding confidence.

"Mr. Jessup, what a surprise!" exclaimed Janet.

"Do you two know each other?" asked the administrator.

"Yes," said Janet carefully. "We have had some business dealings."

"This lady," said Mr. Jessup, "loaned me $7,000 once upon a time to get me started in my business. Without her, I might never have achieved the success I am now enjoying."

"I doubt that," laughed Janet. "You were pretty determined, and I had the feeling nothing would stop you from succeeding."

"Are your children in this school?" Mr. Jessup asked.

"Yes," Janet replied, "both of them. And yours?"

"Yes," said Mr. Jessup. "I wouldn't have them anywhere else. This is the place for children if they are lucky enough to have sensible parents who can afford it. Say, do you have a little time? I have an appointment not too far from here in about an hour. Would you like to join me in a cup of coffee?" They walked to a coffee shop around the corner and enjoyed a wonderful time catching up.

Mr. Jessup eventually agreed to serve as chair of the capital campaign committee and worked tirelessly to see that the auditorium was built and paid for. He worked closely with the architect and involved the whole school community in the design and aesthetics of the facility. When the time came to begin the capital campaign, he was able to enlist a number of area leaders to participate in a media blitz. It featured the unique qualities of the school, the environmentally friendly and beautiful design, and even some of the children's remarkable art and crafts work. The school developed a reputation for its quality of education, and enrollment doubled. In the final days of the capital campaign, when they were still short about $300,000, Mr. Jessup wound up the campaign and celebrated its success by contributing the remaining amount needed.

Janet and Mr. Jessup were standing outside the auditorium building after the dedication ceremony.

"What an amazing series of events this has been," he said. "Who would have thought so many years ago that all of this was in the cards? This whole community was inspired by the possibility of such a building and it has touched all those in its wider area of influence. We dared to dream and then dared to bring it into reality."

"You had a lot to do with it," Janet said, thinking back on their connections and the wonder of how it had all been choreographed from behind the scenes. She suddenly felt overwhelmed with gratitude and tears filled her eyes.

⊷▬▭ ▭▬⊶

I have been involved in many capital campaigns for worthwhile projects. Any tale of success such as this brings back the pure joy of achievement and the same feeling of immense gratitude for what resides in humanity when giving. Giving is the transaction that unites human beings on a higher level. In giving, we almost always feel joined in community toward achieving a social goal that has implications far into the future, and rarely just for ourselves. Even though it is a lonely act, giving comes about in its purest form only when there is a whole community of human beings to receive it and use it for the benefit of us all.

23. THE NATURE OF GIVING

EVERY ONE OF us gives, yet we don't always realize that we are giving. The simple fact that we have children connects us automatically with the stream of giving. Our children enter the world through us, and they are received into the human community. They are a gift in themselves, and through us are given to bring newness and inspiration to our aging world. Without them, we, all of us, would slowly become old and tired and inflexible. Children keep us young, opening our eyes to what is fresh and invigorating in life. In infancy, children are small physically, but they have a whole lot of spirit. How they long to become like us as they struggle to lift their heads, turn their bodies, crawl, stand up, walk, talk, and eventually think. Their unconscious striving is a model of all that is essentially human—the striving to be, to become, to manifest what is in us as a seed.

We feed and clothe our children and give them shelter and guidance and advice and allowances. We give, give, and give some more to our children, to one another, and to the world. Every gift is enabling. It enables a child to grow and become. Whether we have children or not, all of us have been children and experienced this primary element of giving. A gift engenders joy and gratitude, and it appears to be our nature to give. Lending/borrowing and buying/selling are not as intimate to our human nature as is giving and receiving. We love to give and we do it without any training.

From the intimacy of the family, our giving widens to include our community. America has been built on gifts. We would still have our thriving businesses without gifts, but our beautiful natural wonders, parks, and forests would have been ruined long ago if it were not for the incredible philanthropic tradition in this country. There would be no universities, schools, symphony orchestras, theaters, museums, or churches if we had not given generously and continuously. In 2005, well over two trillion dollars were given to non-profits in this country. No other country can match the abundance of such philanthropic outpouring.

What kind of a transaction is giving/receiving? For materialistic thinking, giving is a transaction that doesn't make sense. In order to make it appear more sensible, psychology explains the act of giving as one that must be self-motivated or selfish in some way. It is reasoned that pleasure must occur for a donor in a giving transaction, thus the one who gives must also receive. A donor must get something, or there is no reason to give. What is it that is gotten? Some examples offered are the intangible exchange of pleasure and satisfaction and the gratitude of others, or inscribing a plaque on a building with a family or personal name. Therefore, any gift is just another way to get something. Such materialists cannot conceive of anyone giving something away without an equivalent compensation, and thus they reason that giving and receiving must resemble buying and selling.

All this reasoning denies the existence of our soul and its connection with the spirit. Is it so hard to acknowledge that, living within us, there is a true wish to benefit society and to further what is worthwhile in our culture? Is it too hard to imagine a donor who loves music and thinks it renews the human being to hear a Mozart symphony or a string quartet from another country, and consequently desires to support such events with large donations? Our soul life is renewed and refreshed by most of the charities that receive gifts. A walk in Yosemite National Park fills us with a sense of grandeur and pleasure. Such feelings refresh us; they renew our strength for our daily tasks. A performance of Shakespeare's *Twelfth Night* enlivens us and stimulates our imagination, bringing our souls a multitude of feelings and thoughts. In the middle of a performance, we may even receive a new idea for some problem we are facing in our work or personal life. Such cultural events frequently resolve knots in our relationships through sharing a common experience.

The common view that every gift requires getting is not just cynical; it distorts the truth. It is true that many emotions play into all the transactions that move money, but they don't always supply the motive. Most folks are not wealthy but know such charitable feelings when they give. This is because their gifts are possible only through hard work and struggle. They know what stirs them to sacrifice. They feel something in their souls that urges them to give to a particular cause. For those who are wealthy, a gift to a university to build an auditorium is rarely done just to get the donor's name on the benefactors list. In most cases that I am aware of, being on the benefactors list is nice and offers recognition, but it is not the motive—or let us say it is not enough of a motive to do beneficial sacrificing. Such giving is motivated by some deep feelings of helping an important project, feelings of wanting to serve others through a gift, even feelings of wishing to share some of their good fortune or the fruits of their hard work.

I have a more generous assessment of the human soul and its enormous capacity for giving. Some giving I call "heart giving," because it is inspired by the wish to alleviate human suffering, pain, and worry in others. It is giving of a spontaneous kind. The sight of someone in trouble, in pain, or misery often moves our hearts to do something that will help. To understand giving requires stepping out of the realm of finance and economics and into a new level of ourselves. Giving opens a corner of our souls for more new light and warmth than any other activity we engage in. Even though we must do this for every transaction, with giving/receiving a new dimension enters our consciousness. We are engaged in body, soul, and now spirit. We are moved by our highest intentions. We abandon our concern for immediate, short-term gain and enter the part of us associated with the long-term sustainability and the good of all humankind. We work not only for the true and beautiful in human nature, but also work hand in hand with the "good" in all of us. To understand giving in its true form, we need to involve what is spiritual in us and factor it into the equation of our understanding.

Occasionally, a particular family's story is reviewed in the news, and it usually engenders an outpouring of response and money. For example, some time ago a young hockey player was paralyzed from the neck down as the result of being slammed into the wall during his very first game as a player. The story aired throughout New England, and the donations and service offers poured in from all quarters. Even a special van was partially paid for through additional monetary donations. This is the way we are, because we are a people of heart and reach quickly into our wallets to help others.

Another type of giving is also very prevalent in the United States. When a group of people, a community of purpose, even a whole town, becomes excited about a project from which they all gain, but from which others in the future will also benefit, the assembling of funds is a veritable joy—hard work, but exhilarating. That's what happened in our story "Success." What really happens in such transactions? If we consider the actions that took place in "Success," we can picture a group of people who recognize a certain need such as an auditorium. The solution captures their imagination and fills them with enthusiasm. In their spare time, the group works with architects. They collect all kinds of data and local information about contacts and sources. They visit friends and describe the project. They visit companies in the area and ask for gifts in kind. They ask for windows, doors, lumber, cement, sand, gravel, and hardware—all kinds of gifts in kind for the project. They ask one another for gifts, and they themselves give as much as they are able, some in small amounts, others in larger sums. Something akin to momentum takes hold and carries people along to accomplish incredible results.

In our story, Mr. Jessup had earned and acquired wealth through his ideas and determined action. In spite of his involvement in his business, he was also moved to become involved in the Waldorf school through his children. Their welfare moved him to give his time and energy to the project. Moreover, the new auditorium would serve children and parents for many years to come. He felt inspired by the vision of what such an auditorium would make possible in the community. He was moved to make a very large gift for the long-term benefit of the immediate community and all those still to join them. He felt the thousands of children, some yet to be born, who would one day benefit from such a beautiful building.

Such a moving event as described above always begins with an imagination, a vision that kindles in everyone involved a wish to make it real, to incorporate their imagination into the real world in which they live. At first, the imagination is not in the visible world. It is in their souls. Because it fills them with purpose and excitement, they are energized to fulfill the vision so that everyone, even those who do not have the vision can perceive it with their senses. Put another way, they begin a process of incarnating what is spiritual into what is material. All giving is a matter of enticing spirit into the material world.

What takes a vision, like that of the school in our story, out of the imaginary world, sustained and cherished by living human beings, into the so-called real world? Giving is the magical transaction that incarnates imaginations into the sensory world. Giving is the financial transaction that transforms the invisible into the visible. It is a monetary vehicle for bringing spirit into matter, transforming matter from its natural state and serving the spirit in the human being. Schools, churches, symphony orchestras, to mention a few, are simply structures for supporting the human life of spirit. How can you describe a great symphony? Music is heard, and then it disappears into a void, leaving lingering echoes to remind us of a pleasure that renews us and gives us fresh energy for the conduct of life. What is a wonderful performance of a Shakespeare drama but something that refreshes us, increases our wisdom, and gives us renewed courage to meet our daily responsibilities. These are a few human activities that spring from our cultural life and bring spirit into our daily consciousness. The spirit in us is the force that gives. The spirit in the world is the force that receives.

Now let us consider this question: What is the value of a gift? How do we measure its value, and when is its full value created in time? Let's explore these additional factors in the giving/receiving transaction.

24. The Value of a Gift

THE ACTUAL VALUE of a gift is somewhat mysterious, because nothing is exchanged or gained at the moment of giving. The giving and the receiving are instantaneous, but this transaction does not appear to create an immediate value. It seems to be a transaction that disappears into the world without immediate return benefit. Vincent van Gogh's brother Theo gave him a gift in 1889 to carry Vincent for another seventy days of his life. During that time, Vincent painted seventy paintings, which are now in many museums around the world. Their present value is estimated at hundreds of millions of dollars, virtually priceless. Theo accepted no benefit from the gift, yet we could say Vincent's brother gave a small gift that was eventually worth many millions.

The significant factor in determining the value of a gift is to discover what it makes possible in the future. Its present value cannot really be determined, because no exchange has occurred, nor does a piece of paper exist that fixes a time of repayment or current value, and no repayment is specified. The gift is extraordinarily open-ended, and it expands exponentially into the future. Not only do we look into the future, but also there is no specified consequence. We must wait for an undetermined period to learn of the true value of the gift. The entire transaction has occurred; the gift was made and received without actually creating its real value. The transaction seems to leave physical space entirely, entering time uncertainly to await its full value to render out of the spirit into the full consciousness of humanity. Yet, as we can observe from so many gifts, this transaction appears to be even more productive than the other two. Every gift returns out of the invisible world behind material substance at some undetermined time in the future to bestow a benefit on humanity.

Thus if we want to measure the value of a gift, we must wait for its benefits to materialize at some undetermined time in the future. Not only is the time undetermined; it may be indistinguishable from eternity. What is the quantity of joy and pleasure human beings derive from a van Gogh painting? How long will it give pleasure? The actual value of a gift does not return to the donor, it spreads its forces into the world through the flow of time, never returns, but fructifies our human social life.

To understand the limitless possibilities of the gift consider that we are still unearthing artifacts from civilizations as far back as five millennia and even earlier. A gift to the Waldorf school that leads to building an auditorium might permit countless performances, assemblies, plays, all sorts of cultural events every year for, say, 350 years. What is the value of that? The donor truly sacrifices his or her substance to benefit future humanity. The value of a gift is determined by what it contributes to human progress and renewal. Some might say it could be priceless.

We can say that the value of any gift can never be determined. It literally dies out of material existence never to return except in a different form. It never has an economic value, only a social, spiritual value that sheds light, comfort, joy, and productivity on all humankind. Every gift is a material death and a spiritual birth.

We see that each of these three transaction types has special qualities and characteristics. We will review them and consider how each one can heal some aspect of our social life.

25. THE THREE TRANSACTIONS

THERE ARE THREE transactions and only three, and they all involve two parties. All constitute agreements validated by tangible evidence but motivated by different aspects of our soul. Each affects people and the world differently. Buying/selling draws human beings into the material world and stimulates the whole world to produce what people desire. Lending/borrowing draws human beings into connection with one another, enabling people to accomplish their intentions. It makes the world into a community of striving human beings. Giving/receiving entices the spirit into material existence and can elevate human beings to greater development, wisdom, and love in shaping the future. Based on my observations and experiences, I have concluded that these three transactions are rooted in the architecture of the universe. They contain all the ingredients we need to become healing forces in the life of society. These three transactions are all we need to transform the world, unfold healthy relationships, and reconnect with the active spirit of our time.

I have presented four stories that describe the nature of money as movement through the forces inherent in every transaction. The first, "John's Bargain," describes the buying/selling transaction, reveals its characteristics, and demonstrates how buying/selling moves money quickly and spontaneously. This transaction also draws the human being into the material world. The second story, "Janet's Emancipation," demonstrates how the same transaction requires clear, legally entitled parties that can act as responsible individuals. It raised the questions: What is a responsible individual? And how did we attain that condition of being?

The third story, "Surprise!," presented a surprise when the salesperson suddenly approached John and Janet for a loan. This story introduced the second type of transaction, borrowing/lending. This type of transaction showed completely different characteristics. It transpired over time, seemed mostly to encourage and enable individuals to accomplish personal goals, and drew the parties into relationships that were based on karmic connections and affected their future relationships, even into future lifetimes.

The fourth story, "Success," introduced the giving/receiving transaction. Its characteristics were different from the other two. Both parties were united in their desire to achieve a given project, not for their personal benefit, but for the benefit of future generations with no connection to the parties of the transaction. This transaction benefited future generations and the value of the gift was no longer measurable in material form, but only as spiritual renewal and progress.

All three transactions move money. The movement is quick or slow or even dies out of material existence. The movement has different characteristics, but can be understood only by factoring in the human soul and spirit. Desire (of the soul) fuels the buying/selling transaction; the willingness to help others (a feeling in the soul) accomplish goals forms the basic motivation for the lending/borrowing transaction. The giving/receiving transaction enables people to reach to the highest aspirations (in the soul) for the good of humankind; it becomes a force that brings spirit into reality through the transaction.

It is interesting that, from the point of view of karma, giving relieves the donor but places significant karmic responsibility on the receiver. I wonder if many of us would so easily ask for a gift if we knew its implications for the future. Of course, the fact that we rarely ask for ourselves provides a great protection. We usually request gifts that will somehow benefit many or all of us.

All three transactions involve the soul in some way. The human spirit unites with the spirit of the world through the soul when giving and receiving. The three transactions appropriately fit the basic architecture of the universe and human society. In the next section, we will look at the three basic domains of our human society and explore how money moves in these three domains so that it can be a healing force.

OUR SOCIAL LIFE: THREE IN ONE

26. Our Life with Others

To facilitate healing through money, we relate the movement of money to the evolving human consciousness so that it becomes possible to use common transactions for healing social problems. To do so, we must first examine our social life. If it were possible to divide our life into two parts—one consisting of our private thoughts, feelings, and initiatives and the other of our public statements and actions—we would discover a gray area between the two that often goes unnoticed. In this section, we will consider a little-noticed area that involves the rules of acceptable behavior that we have agreed to follow in our conduct with one another.

I remember a point in my life when I wanted to help students who lacked sufficient funds to attend courses at the Threefold Educational Foundation in Chestnut Ridge, New York.[1] Many students were willing to work for their room, board, and tuition, but jobs were scarce. I had the idea to make wooden toys with students that could be sold, the proceeds of which could be used to help cover their expenses. As soon as I thought the idea through and gained some support from students and faculty, I discovered that there was a kind of social territory between the beginning of an initiative and its realization. The idea itself was inspiring and quickly led to enthusiasm and energy. However, introducing it in a healthy way into the reality of the world demanded a variety of conditions placed on our actions. These conditions came not with the idea, but were imposed on the idea by the world. We had a great many administrative ramifications to be solved. There were questions around the IRS interpretation of such an activity. Then there were technical questions about the equipment and skill needed and the means of payment for work performed.

We understood through this process that an idea or individual initiative is glorious in the head, but when we attempt to imbed it into the world, it has to go through a transitional social structure that involves all kinds of rules and other people's concerns and interests. This led to our understanding that whatever we say or do immediately affects others and leaves behind whatever we considered private. In other words, on the way to becoming an act that affects the physical world, it first influences our social environment.

Every time we want to do something, we are immediately engaged on three levels. First is an idea or impulse to do something. Without this, nothing would ever happen. It is the beginning of all human activity. All our activity begins with a compelling idea that moves us to take action. The second level is what we could call the "translation" level. The idea has to be translated into an actionable plan and process that meets the requirements that the world at its current stage places on us. This includes legal restrictions, social conscience and rules, and all the demands of the human community into which we want to insert our idea. The third level is the action itself, which must occur in accordance with the level of "translation." The action seeks to retain the original inspired idea and manifest the details contained in the idea without violating the social context in which it is to be realized. This requires a kind of "social imagination" to make the idea fit the social environment in which it is planted. This imagination is different from that required by the original idea. It is more practical, more detailed, and includes more process. Whenever we want to do anything, we have to be alive on all three levels. If we are not alive on all three levels and lack the necessary imagination but do not wish to abandon our idea, we had better find help. We are automatically living in a threefold manner when we take any kind of action.

You may associate the word *social* with "fun," like parties, get-togethers, and entertainment. Those are certainly part of what I call our social life, but they are a minor part of our larger social life. "Social life" here means everything we do that affects other human beings. Our social life is what we do in common with others and has social consequences, not only in our relationships, but also in the social "climate" in which we work, interconnect, communicate, and help one another. Our social life is a remarkable structure that can be divided easily into three domains. The three levels from idea to social translation to the action itself are related to the three domains of our social life.

The first domain is *economic,* in that it produces the goods and services we all need to live our lives as we define them. This section mainly discusses the economic domain, but for the sake of clarity we need to identify the two other domains, which are described in later chapters.

The second domain in our social life, which is different but not in conflict with the economic domain, consists of our cultural activity—music, drama, education, reading, writing, singing, and all we do that refreshes and enlightens us to perform our social tasks. Included in this domain are the religious life and many professions such as doctors, teachers, and ministers. Most important, this includes our efforts to obtain creative ideas for understanding or for changing the world.

The third domain is also not at odds with the other two, but again different. It is the whole area of our accepted civil behavior toward one another. It includes our accepted rules governing our actions and the punishments we place on those who do not follow our commonly accepted rules. These rules establish what we consider the rights of any human being within the concept of a lawful society as we currently picture it. The picture we carry of such rights continuously changes, adjusting to changing views of our social life and its rules. The results of all those concepts about individual rights are the laws we impose on one another. These are the three domains in our social life.[2]

We look first at the economic domain. Consider any mature business today; it produces or sells a product or service that generates income at a profit. It typically has a compliance and/or legal department to ensure that it is functioning within the complex network of rules society imposed upon it. Such a business will also have a market research, development, and research department to generate new inspirational ideas for products or services of the future. Coupled closely with these departments is the leadership of the organization, which provides a continual flow of inspiration and new ideas for the management of the enterprise.

I once toured a plant in England with its general manager. We entered a huge room containing two enormous turbines. In the middle of the room was a console from which a single person operated and regulated both machines. The general manager paused as we walked through and addressed the operator.

"What is the temperature in here?" He asked. "It must be at least sixty-eight degrees!"

"That's exactly right, sir," replied the operator.

"How many hours are these turbines in operation?" asked the general manager.

"Twenty-four hours every day of the week, except when one of them is being serviced or repaired."

"Even then you keep the temperature at sixty-eight degrees, don't you?" asked the general manager.

"Of course!"

"Why is it necessary to keep the temperature at sixty-eight? These turbines generate heat, and couldn't they function at a lower temperature?" He asked.

"Yeah, but we couldn't. At any moment we might have to respond quickly. Besides, we stand here on four-hour shifts, and a low temperature would affect our health. Please sir, don't think of lowering the temperature."

"I wasn't thinking of lowering the temperature," replied the general manager, smiling. "I was thinking of enclosing this console and ten cubic feet with a heated structure for the operator. Then we could lower the temperature of the rest of the space. This must be about 400,000 cubic feet. It would cost a lot less to heat ten cubic feet than to heat 400,000 cubic feet, wouldn't you say?"

The operator rubbed his chin and agreed dubiously.

"Well, think about it. You may know of some reasons why it wouldn't work. Maybe it is too expensive or technically too hard on the turbines or whatever. Let's think about it. I'll talk with you later."

We moved on through the plant and he muttered to me, "I don't understand why nobody thinks of these things. In a year we might be able to save thousands of dollars, conserve energy, even make it more comfortable for an employee, and still get the same performance out of the turbines."

The person, who does the least amount of physical work, may contribute greatly to the success of an enterprise by contributing ideas. In this example, the general manager had the good idea, and although he had the power to make the decision on the spot, he knew the idea needed to go through the translation phase before acting on it. He wasn't about to order a change without complete consideration of the second level of social life, the restrictions and rules imposed by the social context. However, he had seen the advantages and would no doubt press for action after considered investigation of all relevant factors. This example illustrates how the threefold nature of human activity plays out in practice and how idea is translated and eventually executed within its appropriate bounds.

Every human being must be cognizant of these three levels of social life leading to social action. No organization can be successful unless it organizes itself in a threefold manner. It must organize to receive inspired ideas and it must organize to fit into the legal and societal structure of the land. It must also organize to translate inspiration into action that will serve its customers.

We will explore these three elements and how they are reflected in the three transaction types, buying/selling, lending/borrowing, and giving/receiving. These three transaction types are not arbitrary; they are as much a part of the architecture of human society as are the three levels, from idea to action, and the three domains I will abbreviate as "business," "government," "and "education." These three terms for the three areas of our social life are a kind of shorthand for quick reference; they are each much more complicated than the word typically indicates. We will look at each in detail. Healing through money requires us to understand how money circulates through the three domains of our social life, so that healing is consistent with the basic architecture of current day society. Let us now consider the role of business in our social life, what it contributes, how it maintains itself, and its underlying function in our society.

27. BUSINESS IS SERVICE

T HE MINUTE I started the toy-making activity at the Threefold Educational Foundation, we learned the hard way to distinguish between economic work and education. We decided to make beautiful wooden puzzles. Much creativity went into designing them and determining the most cost-effective way to produce them. We were able to jigsaw them out of basswood plates ten at a time. Any more than that caused distortions in the resulting puzzle pieces. Each puzzle piece was then colored with non-toxic dyes. This had to be done by hand. The first student looked at the beautiful colors and the final picture that would result from her work and was delighted. She started her work with considerable enthusiasm. Of course the first one or two had a few anomalies, not real flaws, but differences, shall we say, from the pattern.

By the tenth puzzle, the end of a single set, this student was acquiring the skill and enjoying her work. She looked with pleasure at the next pile of ten puzzles to color. She was paid by the puzzle and thought what a wonderful thing to be paid for doing such beautiful work. She felt truly fortunate and plunged ahead enthusiastically. She completed the next set of ten and then a third set of ten. Remarkably enough she completed the third set in about half the time it took her to do the first. She sat at the table and cut quite a dashing, confident figure as she splashed color on each piece, rubbed it for the right effect, and swiftly moved on to the next piece. She was clearly on top of her job.

About the third afternoon of working on the same puzzle, she had completed her ninth set of ten puzzles. She had hand painted ninty puzzles. I was there when we placed before her the tenth set for her to color. She looked at us somewhat balefully, I thought, and wondered whether there wasn't another puzzle with a different picture for her to color. I realized she had come to a certain threshold in her will forces. She had come to the end of her enthusiasm and was now in a more serious phase. I reminded her that her first few puzzles were not exactly perfect, that she was learning all along the way and now, finally, she had arrived at the point where she was no longer learning, but producing cost-effectively with what we hoped the children would enjoy playing.

At this point we assembled all the students working on the toys to process what was going on. An understanding developed among us that learning is exciting and that applying the new skills can be thrilling. Economic value is not yet generated until this first "honeymoon" phase of production is over. When we entered economic production, a new connection had to be established with the reasons for producing something at all. The students then took some of the puzzles to homes with children, saw them play with the puzzles, and connected with the pleasure that the children had with what they had made. After that, every time their enthusiasm flagged, the antidote was to visit children playing with their puzzles. This shows that, at heart, the very nature of all business is to serve. We don't produce for ourselves. It is an error to think that we work to earn a living for ourselves. Earning a living and supporting our families is important. It may even work as a motive. However, what we are actually doing is serving others.

The French Revolution introduced the trinity of liberty, fraternity, and equality. Fraternity is embedded in the deeper nature of the economic element of our social life. The very essence of any economic enterprise is, as it should be, to serve the needs of others. It supports all human beings, not just a special group or only a few of us, but all humankind. Business is the Atlas or Hercules on whose shoulders the welfare of humankind rests. Thus any business that does not serve a human need of some kind has either to create a desire for what it offers or stop making it. Why else would businesses run market surveys and constantly seek the opinions of customers about their products or services. They need to know whether they are serving a need in the best possible way and whether their customers are still satisfied. Of course, business often manipulates the market to gain an advantage.

Not all products are objectively "good" for us. Businesses are not responsible for what some people might think is "good" or "not good." Their task is to satisfy their customers and give them what they are willing to purchase. Business generally leaves the question of what is "good" for people to the other two domains of the social organism. The domain of education is looked to for changing people and their so-called needs and desires, and the domain of government is looked to for questions of compliance and rights.

As humankind continues to mature and develop, we will demand healthier products and practices. Businesses will change because they respond with alacrity to the changing demands of individuals and groups of human beings. Even if businesses try to influence us through the media and advertising, pretending that whatever they produce is good for us, our development is reaching a point of independent judgment. Think of the change surrounding social smoking. When I was in my teens, I never thought about health at all, and I smoked for its effect on what I thought was my image. My grandchildren look at me in horror when I tell them how ignorant I was when I smoked. To them the facts are so clear.

Gradually, the social impulse to support all human beings, which is inherent in the economic realm of our social life, will manifest and reveal itself. Increasingly, we will demand what is healthy for us for our lives together and for the Earth on which we live. Business will continue to serve us and meet our needs. It is up to us the consumers to create the demands that further our development, our health, and our quality of life. We mustn't expect business to do our demanding for us.

Moreover, how do businesses serve us in producing the products and services we ask for and consume? Businesses utilize as fully as possible the human capacities they find in their employees. They actually consume human capacities to provide the products and services we need and demand. Try visiting an employment office with this line: "I have been a teacher of English all my life and I have been wondering what it is like to be an accounting clerk in business. I am intelligent, a hard worker and can learn very fast. I'd like to apply for a position as an accounting clerk in your organization." It is very unlikely that you will be hired. You will be advised to take courses in accounting, get a degree or diploma in bookkeeping or accounting, obtain a job in some other organization for a while, and then come back and apply. This is not necessarily a cruel or bad approach. Their task in our social life is not to further the development of human capacities. Their task is to use up, to consume, human capacities to provide the best products and services at the lowest cost.

Of course, companies provide training programs that train employees how to do a specific task or learn certain complementary skills needed for expected job performance. Sometimes companies find employees who are defective in certain necessary skills and may supplement their normal education with additional courses. However, companies do this simply because they have to get the most out of every employee. Moreover, I say rightfully so. Business should focus entirely on providing us with the goods and services we require. That in itself is a big enough job, so long as they provide their employees with safe, humane working conditions and promote the healthy environment we all need for living together. More and more emphasis is now placed on the cost of avoiding processes and equipment that damage our environment. Providing us with goods and services at an affordable cost is becoming increasingly difficult and requires all the ingenuity of everyone involved in the economic life.

Does any employee of a business have a right to a certain job for life? The minute we ask about employees' rights, we are in a different domain of our social life. What are our rights? How are they made universal? What constitutes compliance? These questions belong in another domain, which I refer to as "government." It's the rightful function of government to look across the board through all social life to ensure the rights of every individual as defined and accepted by all of us at any given time.

Can any employee demand joy and pleasure from work? Should an employee continually experience new insights and new skills in the job? Should an employee demand growth and development? The minute we speak about learning, enthusiasm, joy, and development of new capacities we approach another domain of our social life, the one I call "education," which draws our potential out of us. Except for what it needs to produce products and services, it is not the function of business to develop human capacities.

A healthy social life does not mean that everyone does everything; rather, the essential characteristics of each domain must be clearly understood and differentiated, with collaboration across the board. In chapters 31 and 32, we will learn more about this and how collaboration among the three domains can enhance our social life. We will also investigate the domains of government and education to complete our picture, though in a somewhat simplified way, of the threefold architecture of our social life.

28. WEALTH:
A BYPRODUCT OF BUSINESS

A BYPRODUCT OF BUSINESS is both profit and wealth. Capital arises from the vast differentiation of our work, which we will explore further in the following chapter. We focus first on the economic life of our social organism, not because it is most important, but because it is so prominent in our consciousness today. In the social organism of our time, the economic element, with its focus on the physical needs of everyone, enables a great many of us to live and prosper in an environment conducive to our development.

Unfortunately, the acquisition of means does not always allow its owners to develop and render greater service to humanity. Frequently, wealth becomes a kind of drug to which people grow addicted and find themselves cut off from the rest of humanity. I was recently in a hotel in Mexico City for a conference. It was an extremely comfortable hotel with several restaurants, an indoor pool, a ballroom, conference rooms, and exercise rooms. In spite of the amenities, several in our group wanted to go out and enjoy a particular restaurant they knew, and I joined them. As we exited the main lobby and strolled down a walkway to waiting taxis, a number of poor people swarmed into the walkway and offered us iguanas and jewelry for sale before they were chased back into the shadows. I remember it, because I lost my appetite and returned alone to the hotel, which turned out to be no real comfort.

We who are better off economically are sometimes insulated from the true struggle of people to survive and become more human. Wealth, or even partial wealth, often leads to wanting more and better accoutrements of "good living," which in turn does not seem to lead to greater happiness and enjoyment of life. It seems impossible to satisfy the appetite for more things, gadgets, and food, larger houses, more land, and grander cars. The more we have the more we want. There is always someone who has more and whom we envy and want to match. Those few who actually enjoy their acquired means quickly learn that a simple life provided with basics usually offers the best opportunity for enjoyment, happiness, peace, and unity with others.

"Making it" often refers to the acquisition of wealth and a host of necessary and unnecessary things. It is a hard lesson to learn, but almost all learn it in time; simplicity leads to joy, and wealth leads to isolation and mistrust. Imagine being afraid to walk the streets on an evening without a bodyguard. Imagine not knowing for sure whether you have a friend or only someone who is attracted to your wealth. Neither is being poor the answer. Being poor involves feeling all the aspects of poverty. The Franciscan monk who relies on others to put food into his bowl does not feel poor. He feels unencumbered. Being poor usually means *feeling* poor and lacking the capacity to know where to turn for help. Very often, feeling poor is coupled with feeling unwanted, abandoned, and without hope.

Even Henry David Thoreau, who set out to prove that one could live very simply on very little and still have a worthwhile life, lived in this way for only a short while just to prove his point, and, even so, escaped occasionally for dinner. No, the answer is not being poor or feeling poor, as so many people today must experience. To live with sufficient means is the answer. Such a life has the least stress and the greatest peace. Thoreau's book *Walden* was named after Walden Pond, where he lived very simply for more than a year. It enlightened us on this piece of wisdom fourteen decades ago, but it had little effect on the forward thrust of our accumulating thirst for "things."

Business is not at fault for this human illness today. Although it is spurred on through advertising and the media, it is not really the cause, but only the party taking advantage of an existing weakness in our souls. We demand what is advertised. We permit the influence of the media in our lives. In the end, business and the media are not satisfied with a course that does not get results. Are we beginning to have enough strength to forge a life that we ourselves determine? Do we now even consider which values are important to us, and do we act on them free of surrounding influences and inner urges? When we shop around for the cheapest eggs, do we ask what our actions tell farmers about our needs? Can we blame them for creating egg factories with several thousand chickens crammed twenty-four hours a day into a building so tightly that no chicken can move or sit except on their roosting shelves where egg laying is their "job?" What are our values, and how do we communicate them to producers and businesses?

First we focus on business and the economic domain of our social life, bearing in mind that business is not everything in our social life. We will consider the life of rights and the cultural life in chapters 31 and 32. We will see how the economic domain affects the life of rights and the life of culture in the following story, "Young Smart." It is a compressed version of what happened over the hundreds of years leading up to the industrial revolution and beyond, characterizing very briefly the division of labor, from its roots to modern labor in its disconnected form. Modern labor provides greater efficiency, less satisfaction, more profit, and an explosion of wealth for the few with initiative and luck.

29. YOUNG SMART

YOUNG SMART LIVED in the small village of Ochinia in Central Europe. He delighted in observing everything that went on in the village, and nothing escaped his attention. Sometimes his fellow villagers told him in no uncertain terms to buzz off, asking why he had nothing to do but to watch others work. He was nevertheless far from discouraged, and as he grew out of his late teens and into manhood, he not only watched everything that went on, but also asked questions about everything he saw happening.

"Why does it take so long to hammer iron into a tool? Why do you have to hammer it, place it back into the furnace, hammer it again, and repeat the process so many times? Can't you skip a few steps?" With these questions, he would be chased away by the smithy.

"Why do you bake only six loaves at a time? Couldn't you use a larger oven and bake twelve at a time?" he asked the baker. He received hoots of laughter from the baker, who had learned baking from her parents, who had in turn learned it from their parents.

"Couldn't we run a trough through the village to bring water to the stables instead of carrying it from the well in large buckets? Wouldn't it be easier and save someone's back for other work?" he asked the stable boys. The villagers continually told him there was no work for the likes of him; without a trade and without any other tasks to perform, how would he support himself and be useful in the village?

In time the village prospered and grew into a veritable town with a much larger population, all employed gainfully in one task or another. Young Smart had lately taken an interest in the shoemaker and his work. He asked many questions and, although he had never cut out any leather, prepared it for sewing, sewed it, and shaped a shoe, he knew every single step, from hide to shoe.

The shoemaker had special status in the town. He knew every one of his customers, the shoes they were wearing, and their tasks in life.

He often spoke of his deeper mission: "Your feet take you through life. They take you away from where you shouldn't be and toward where your destiny is fulfilled. I create shoes to help people fulfill their destinies. To do that, you have to know the kind of person for whom you create shoes. You have to understand their innermost drives and their dreams and longings to be fulfilled in the course of their travels and meandering." The shoemaker believed his trade was somehow blessed work, and it caused him deep satisfaction when he was successful in helping others achieve their goals in life. Imagine his surprise when Young Smart came to him one day and offered him a proposition.

"If I bring you a number of hides, all cut out for a hundred different size and styles of shoes, will you sew them together into shoes?"

The shoemaker thought Young Smart was mad. "Why would I do that?" he demanded.

"Why? Because for every pair of shoes you sew together for me, I will pay you two drachmas. For one hundred shoes you will earn two hundred drachmas, and you could sew a hundred shoes in one week."

"That's more than I earn in two weeks," mused the shoemaker. "But what good would the shoes be? Who would want to wear them? Shoes are for a particular person, not for any old foot! Moreover, who will prepare the hides? And who will polish and lace the shoes? And who will fit into them?"

"Those are all my worries and my concerns. I will see to those details. You do your part, I will take care of the rest," said Young Smart.

"But they won't fit anybody!" The shoemaker shouted in exasperation.

Young Smart replied. "Out of a hundred shoes, each pair is bound to fit someone."

"Just anybody?"

"Yes," said Young Smart.

"I won't do it!" insisted the shoemaker.

Young Smart left and talked to other shoemakers, with more or less the same response. The shoemaker thought about Young Smart's proposition. He knew that his roof leaked from time to time that his wife had only one good dress, and his children often had very little to eat. Two hundred drachmas could make a difference. Whether Young Smart could use the shoes and find people to fit into them was not really something that needed to concern him. His part of the task was just to sew together whatever parts he was given. A very stupid way to make shoes, but for the sake of two hundred drachmas, he was tempted. After all, he could still make shoes for his cherished customers and fulfill his mission in life and do this on the side or at night.

The next time Young Smart came around and pressured the shoemaker with his proposition, the shoemaker asked many more questions and eventually agreed, even though his whole nature rebelled against this way of making shoes. He couldn't grasp how anybody would want to wear a shoe made in this way.

He was happy to receive two hundred drachmas once he had sewn together the hundred pieces of hide into rough shoes, turned them over to Young Smart, and hoped he would never see him again. He bought a new dress for his wife, shopped for some wonderful food, and they celebrated their good fortune.

"Can you just imagine what Young Smart is going to do with a hundred shoes that do not fit anyone?" He laughed and his whole family laughed uproariously with him.

Young Smart had found others to process and cut up the hides. He also found someone to finish off the shoes, add laces and buckles, polish them and package them nicely in colored boxes and ribbons. He borrowed a cart, arranged them so they were clearly visible from all sides, and began to move about town, calling out the virtues and low prices of his shoes. At first, many of the villagers laughed at him, and some even threw stones at him, but gradually some found that they liked a particular style, color, and price. Within a month, most of the shoes had been sold.

Young Smart had kept careful records of all his expenses and all his income in a black book with columns. He knew exactly where every penny went and where his income came from. At the end of the month, he totaled all his expenses and his income and was relieved to discover that his income was greater than his expenses. It seemed like a miracle. A hundred shoes could be made less expensively by dividing up the work among many people and paying them all more than they could earn by making shoes themselves. It gave many people work that was less interesting, to be sure, but it gave them more income and in the end returned a profit to the organizer and manager of the enterprise. He made plans for the future with a light heart and an iron will to launch his experiment into a full-scale enterprise that would spread to other towns as well.

30. WE GAINED AND LOST

WHAT ARE YOUR observations about this story? Do you see what was won and what was lost? Do you recognize the shoemaker's loss? He traded work that was deeply satisfying and required all his masterful skill as an artisan for fragmented work that required less skill but provided a larger compensation. In a way, we could say that he sold his soul. And who can blame him? He and his family were deprived of many things. They were surviving, but just barely.

These developments happened quite differently in real time, stretching over the more than two hundred years of industrial revolution. Nevertheless, it can be useful to look at it in compressed form as a simple story. Mostly, history is studied and presented to us in such detail that we lose sight of the underlying movement in the story. In the end, we think there is no story or movement, but only a welter of occurrences and reactions that lead nowhere.

In the early 1800s, particularly in England, large "sweatshops" were established in which people worked by the piece. Together with that development, all kinds of machines were invented. The sewing machine made it possible for individuals to cut out patterns, others to sew them together, still others to wash, fold, and pack them into bundles of uniform clothes sent to retail markets. Soon there were many tasks requiring little skill, and children as young as five or six were employed. The rights of human beings were violated, but no compliance was demanded. As a people, we were asleep to the common rights now accorded every person.

In the United States, sweatshops were part of the landscape of the industrial revolution. If you visit almost any town in New England, you can see the many mills now turned into shopping malls. In Amsterdam, New York, you will see mills where weavers worked, but were replaced gradually by enormous mechanical looms. Even during the late 1950s, vocational schools in Amsterdam still taught weaving and how to operate the early looms, though they had become obsolete as centrally operated machines came into use for manufacturing fabric. The business had long ago moved out, and the town was struggling to survive economically. Gradually the mills were turned into condominiums and shopping malls. Wander through any such town and you will see evidence of the story of Young Smart spread out in the town—two hundred years of the industrial revolution compressed into a single town.

Most artisans today have to deal with the consequences of the industrial revolution. They can rarely charge as much as they should for their labor and usually have to take part-time or nighttime jobs to keep up with their expenses. I have a friend who inherited a trust fund and decided to "return to the land." He purchased a farm in Vermont and moved in with some friends. They decided not to rely on machinery but use their own hands and simple tools. It was not a matter of money, but one of principle. Chain saws wreck havoc with the mess, the noise, and the pollution they create in the woods. Their experiment lasted only a year, and I saw very little change in the place. True, it was quiet and peaceful, but the tree trunks that had been cut down with an ax were piled beside the barn. One field was cleared, but two others down the road still had the cut grass lying on top of the stubble waiting to be gathered as hay into the barn. The stalls in the cow barn were empty except for a heifer in one of the pens.

I asked my friend, now alone on the premises, why he was selling the property after just one year. He told me the whole long story and ended by saying, "There is something in the world today that you can't fight. None of us are strong enough to go up against the machines. We, the human race, have lost the battle against another mass invasion, the machine." There is something sad about this situation, and yet we can't turn back the clock, nor do we really want to, because we are convinced we need much more than earlier economic conditions would have provided. It isn't really greed; it's just our longing for a reasonably "good" life.

Young Smart, who early in his life was considered somewhat useless, turned out to have one capacity, which he had in spades. He poured his intelligence into how things are made. He had the ability to organize other people's labor. He directed his given spiritual capacity into the material world and found "better" ways to do things. By "better" we mean making things in such a way that no soul work was needed.

Anyone, who expects to derive deep satisfaction from an industrial job today expects something that is no longer possible. True, you can make your job palatable through social connections, conversations with others, and complaining about the boss. However, it's rarely possible to feel in your heart that your work is truly important and that you are contributing to the wellbeing of humanity.

As a result, we began to have workers who were asked to render only minor skills and leave their souls at home. They were expected to pick up their souls on the way home, dust them off, and entertain them with canned music, moving pictures, sex, and alcohol. Work that involves souls and gives satisfaction was no longer considered valuable. It marked the end of an era and the beginning of social problems with workers. The only thing left was to organize and fight for more money, with the idea that this would make up for the loss of soul satisfaction. It never did. Young Smart never looked back. He was not concerned with questions of long-term improvement for humanity. He was thrilled with his own intelligence and all that it could do; he felt it was a nifty device to pour out into the world.

Have you ever asked yourself what a machine really is? Think about it. We know every detail of how it is made and how every part functions and connects with every other part. We have an overview of its entirety, because we created it. It's not like a plant that grows out of the vast wisdom of nature. It is a movable object created by us. How did we create it? We poured our intelligence into a problem and then poured our intelligence into the solution. Every part of a machine is like our intelligence, frozen into matter to serve our purpose in a mechanical way. Machines are like a mirror of our own intelligence. The telephone is a kind of imitation of our larynx and ear. The threshing machine is an imitation of how we used to beat the grain out of the straw. Because our intelligence is frozen into machines, we understand them entirely. We comprehend everything about them, or at least we can if we try. We are able to understand almost everything about any machine, much more than we know about a chipmunk or a skunk. There is something in every animal or plant that is still a mystery to us, but the machine has nothing to hide from our intelligence.

Young Smart convinced himself rather quickly that he was doing something very good. He was raising the economic standard of poor people. He even gave work to some that formally had performed only menial tasks. Not much intelligence was required when you divided all the work into little parcels. Young Smart supplied all the intelligence needed for the enterprise to prosper. Wonder of all wonders, as the enterprise grew and developed, a surplus appeared almost by magic. In no time, he had what was later to be referred to as "capital." The division of labor seems to result in the creation of capital. So how does capital come about? Every time we apply our spiritual capacities to the material world, without soul or concern for humanity and our long-term future, we are rewarded with increasing capital.

What do you think Bill Gates did to earn his billions? Do you think he really rolled up his sleeves and worked as sweat poured down his face? Not at all; he worked all right, but with his mind. He devoted all his spiritual capacities to finding a way for human intellectual skills to be mechanized. He couldn't do it for anything creative, but he found a way to mechanize the intellect's analytical and calculating skills. Consider how he poured his greatest intellectual gifts into the operating system that is used in computers almost everywhere. His reward for sacrificing his spirit was billions of dollars. When Bill Gates chose to donate many billions of dollars to the foundation he created and later, with help from Warren Buffet, began to work on how to improve the world with seventy billion dollars, he may have realized the sacrifice he made. The sacrifice was made when he poured his sacred intelligence into the creation of Windows software. Fortunately, he has great spiritual gifts and may discover how to renew them through this new task. After all, benefiting humanity is still the function of business. Regardless of whether you call it a foundation, serving others is still a kind of business. If Bill Gates decides to break new ground and investigate new ways to deal with poverty, ill health, and ignorance, then he will have left the domain of business and entered the domain of education.

I am not condemning Young Smart or Bill Gates. I see all the great advantages and benefits that have accrued to a certain number of people. However, you have to admit that, as human beings, we never asked which quality of life is best for human beings. It has always been assumed that more food, more clothes, faster word processors, bigger houses, and more fun are inevitably better for everyone. Surely a gold-plated Cadillac can't really be better than a simpler, more functional car, or even a hybrid car, in these days of higher gasoline prices.

Only now is the great disparity among people beginning to surface. Why is it surfacing now? It has always been there, but we are now far more aware of it. Our changing consciousness is beginning to take into account the serious conditions of poverty that so many have to endure in various parts of the world. The media bring everything into our home and have contributed greatly to our change in consciousness. In medieval times, there was even greater disparity, but people were less conscious and generally accepted their fate. When Charles Dickens brought attention to the dire conditions among many of the children in the industrial age through his fiction, which appeared in newspapers as serial stories, the populace was stirred to action. As soon as people roused themselves, governments began to wake up and focus on new rules. The industrial revolution worsened the lot of many children, but it also brought about increased consciousness and government legislation.

Now we find that life has paid a dirty trick on us. We cannot go back, and we are wary of moving forward along the same trajectory. It has become obvious that too many of us suffer in poverty. Worldwide, the number is staggering. Too many of us derive little soul nourishment from our daily work; ask any hourly laborer whether the daily job is satisfying. Too many people lack an enlivening education. I recently asked an acquaintance why so many children dislike going to school. His answer surprised me: "School is not there to enjoy; it's something you have to suffer through until you graduate." If you recall, that was also John's view of education until he discovered Waldorf education, which allows and encourages children to love what they are doing.

Further, too many of us are lost in debilitating modes of entertainment. In our spare time, we should be able to refresh ourselves so that we have renewed energy for life's tasks. After an evening of television and drinking in a local sports bar, or at home in the den, we usually feel more drained. Thank God no one has mechanized sleep, yet. Finally, too many of us are aware of everything going on around us in the world, but feel impotent to do anything about what we see. We feel manipulated by an unseen force that seems to drive our civilization toward inevitable crisis and destruction. In work groups and meetings, people sometimes ask me, "Who's in charge?" Buckminster Fuller described the Earth as a kind of spaceship hurtling through vast spaces, with no one at the helm. His point was to encourage us to begin to feel responsible and to grow in capacity so that we can take charge more and more. Is it time for that? I think it is!

In spite of this, I don't think we should despair when positive action seems to take forever, and everything appears to be getting worse. Sometimes things have to get really bad, much worse than they are, before we find the inner forces to take up the challenge and start a new trend toward healing ourselves and our Earth. The problem is that the causes for all the so-called social ills emanate from us. We are the ones who cause pollution and global warming. We clog our waste dumps, make our cities filthy, fill our streams and waterways with artificial fertilizers, and serve beautiful food with little nutritional value. We are the ones who believe that computers are the foundation of a good education. We have given in to a kind of slovenliness. We need to change, but until our backs are really against the wall, we may not feel the need to change. It may not occur to us that, with each day, that wall moves a little closer. If we wake up to the power of every financial transaction to transform the world, empower individuals, and draw inspiration and spiritual insight into our affairs, we will begin to take charge. It's certain that no one else will. We are the ones!

We are causing the problems, but we have the capacity to "see," to think the solutions, feel the enthusiasm for change, and the will to transform our personal and social life. Our threefold nature can join seamlessly with the threefold nature of our social life and transform it to reflect our values. How do we do this? We instill every transaction with increased consciousness.

I believe every financial transaction contains the rudiments of social healing. When we wake up to this and begin to pour our spiritual capacities and values into every transaction, the world will change for the better. Each of us as individuals will take part in awakening consciousness of the movement of money. That is why some of us gathered in 1981 to begin a process of working with money in a new way. We wanted to bring the emerging human consciousness into a responsible relationship with money and to see how we can use it to change the way the world works with money. Out of that impulse, we created the Rudolf Steiner Foundation (RSF) and poured our spiritual and social intentions into its mission and organizational life. In section seven, we will look more closely at this organism for change and healing.

31. OUR THREE-DIMENSIONAL SOCIAL LIFE

L ET'S TRY TO get a better understanding of the three domains of our social life so that we can begin to work with healing in whatever domain challenges us. I am referring to our economic life, our life of rights, and our cultural life, which I have called business, government, and education. Rudolf Steiner, in his lectures and books, originally identified these three domains of our social life, which are not new and exist today. To move forward from the present point it will help to understand that, although the three are intertwined and overlap, they have separate functions in our social life.

If any of the three domains becomes weak, all become less effective. If any become too dominant and overrun one or both of the others, we all suffer and human social life as a whole is damaged. Balance and clarity are highly desirable and will develop gradually as they should. I do not despair of what the future will bring, because I have such confidence in what I see emerging in human beings. It will involve pain and revelation, but it will also heal our present social ills. I have a very long-term view of our evolution.

The governmental function in our social life does *not* have to do with providing goods and services. The fact that the government runs more than five hundred businesses demonstrates how poorly it is equipped for that function. Government is supposed to struggle for the rights of every single human being. It has to guarantee those rights and adjust as the implementation of those rights changes. Today we recognize that every human being has a right to an education that prepares a person for life. Government rightly supports that right and does all it can to ensure that no individual child has to do without. The function of government is *not* to determine what constitutes an appropriate education for any child, but to see that every child receives an education.

The establishment of standardized examinations, for example, and using government grants to force teachers to teach according to them is inappropriate for any government. You may ask how we should maintain standards. One answer is that this is certainly not the government's function. The influence of government, whether deliberately so or simply the result of its nature, arbitrarily forces equality into the curriculum and teaching. It is abundantly clear that every child is unique and will grow and learn according to the child's own development; nonetheless, government insists that all children must acquire certain skills at given ages. The only way to insist on such a program is to maintain the lowest, most common levels of learning so that the majority, at least, conforms. We may be attempting to develop automatons, but children will simply not conform. The best are most likely to give the most trouble.

While the economic realm of our social life has brotherhood at its roots, the equality of all human beings is the essence of good government. The right of a child to an education is universally accepted today. What is not understood is that the right to an education does not specify the nature of that education. Educators must take this cause to heart. Determining what constitutes an appropriate education for each individual child may be different in some areas than it is in others. That was how education functioned in the past. As the result, a gifted individual such as Abraham Lincoln was not compelled to endure an uninspired, mediocre education. He could proceed at his own speed and develop his unique capacities, which benefited everyone.

This brings us to the third domain of a healthy social organism: the spiritual/cultural life. All art, education, research, and religious aspiration belong to this domain. This includes all that renews and refreshes and prepares human beings to serve one another and human evolution as a whole. There must be freedom in this domain, because we are all different and unequal in the sense that each of us has certain unique capacities unlike those of any other person. Each of us has to be free to develop our own capacities to the highest potential in us. In this domain of our common social life, we need to celebrate our differences, enjoy one another's uniqueness, and grant every individual the right to develop and prosper according to one's own capacities and aspirations.

These are the three fundamental domains of modern social life. I refer to them as business, government, and education. In his lectures and writings on the threefold social order, Rudolf Steiner called them economic life, rights life, and cultural life. Each is different and yet they each overlap and intermingle with the others. Economic enterprise serves everyone and fosters brotherhood. Government guarantees each of us certain rights and ensures equality under the law. Government must fight against unequal treatment of individuals; it bases its mission on the domain that makes us equal, our rights as individuals. The spiritual/cultural domain of humanity is ruled by absolute freedom and offers us each the opportunity to develop our individual capacities to the highest possible level.

It will become increasingly important to our development not to confuse these three domains, even though they must collaborate and function together seamlessly. Mainly, the leadership in each area must understand the differences of each realm and honor the functions of the others. Confusion leads only to abuses in any of the three areas. For example, as mentioned, when government deals in education, it has a tendency to bring all levels of achievement to a single, lower standard, which is easer to measure and teach. Standards tend to become equality of learning rather than excellence fitted to the individual.

Imagine the government insisting that everyone who plays the piano should have an equal right to perform in a symphony hall. In the realm of culture, we are singularly unequal, and it is up to each of us to determine how we shape our lives and use our talents. When the education, or spiritual/cultural, domain gets involved in the rights of human beings, it tends to ignore common rights and to favor those who are more endowed. Imagine only the very intelligent and most gifted being permitted to develop their talents to the fullest. All human beings must have the opportunity to develop their own inherent capacities. Who can assess the value of a potential carpenter as more or less valuable to society than a potential scientist? They are both needed and, because they have rights as individuals, each should be permitted to develop uniquely through an education that cherishes their individuality. Freedom in this domain ensures the spiritual advancement of all human beings.

When the economic domain begins to dominate our social life, it tends to overuse people and manipulate them by appealing too strongly to their unsatisfied desires. Would it not be shocking if a very talented musician or artist cannot be heard or seen because it is not profitable? Perhaps the music of Joseph Haydn is no longer as popular as it used to be. If a composition by him does not fill all the seats, should it be eliminated from concert programs? If people leave and refuse to hear it, then the orchestra has to bow to its economic constraints. If it were purely a business, orchestras would only play the ten most popular compositions, and we would have a classical hit parade. Business must stick to its functional domain in society, which is to satisfy human physical needs.

The three domains of our social life are also reflected in the three transactions that bring about the movement of money. I'm sure that this is not surprising. Buying/selling is largely the transaction that fuels the economic domain of our social organism. Borrowing/Lending is more the transaction that supports community life and makes possible the adjustments that guarantee everyone's basic rights. Someone who has a truly good idea, an awareness of social connections and constraints, and the right technical capabilities should not be prevented from acting because financial resources are lacking. Somehow, through lending and borrowing, all practical, useful ideas should be fundable. This doesn't always happen today. However, more people have access to loans than ever before because of the emergence of micro lending, which provides small loans to assist a small group of people to start local businesses. Lending smoothes over economic differences, links people in projects and social activity, and enables those with less to make use of the resources of those with more. In fact, all financial transactions tend to be correctly associated with the life of rights in our social organism. Giving/Receiving, although very helpful in smoothing out some of the disparities among human conditions, belongs mostly with the cultural aspect, which includes education, the arts, research, and spiritual nourishment. Let's look more closely at the third domain, education, and its role in our social life.

32. OUR CULTURAL LIFE

S CHOOLS, COLLEGES, AND churches serve different functions in society than does government or business. A building for a school is a place for renewing life, for bringing the children who will change the world into our social life. A school can be a center for social renewal, although I know most of us don't think of it that way. We seem to think of it as a place where facts are drilled into stubborn minds and where certain limited skills are demanded. The battle cry of reading, writing, and arithmetic still resounds throughout our educational system, with a slight harmonic addition of civic education so that children will know enough to vote when they reach the proper age. These basics are essential, but even if that's all schools are supposed to achieve, they generally fail. The latest pedagogical idea is to educate children earlier while they are still malleable and too innocent to resist. "Give me a child before the age of seven, and I will have him for life" was the motto of a certain prominent church. It could easily be the motto for our educational institutions.

Reading in kindergarten is a crime against childhood. Reading and other disciplines have crept into the early years largely because the learned educators don't know what else to do. They don't realize the value of play, experience, and exploration. They think that, unless they teach something, children won't learn anything. It is incredibly arrogant to think that learning and development take place only when adults are teaching children. Have you ever watched a small group of young children play in a large apple tree? Not only are they developing all sorts of coordination and muscle development, but also their eyes are maturing and learning to guide them through the intricate lacework of branches. They are learning when to pause and plan and when to move. A few boards in the tree can become a platform for developing further strategies. To an adult, such a platform may seem to be only a crude construction, but to children it can be a fort or castle in the sky with distant views and oversight on the activity of other children who may be archers or warriors or foreign critics. With young children in an apple tree, all things are possible. Much formal learning comes too early and too fast and too shallow for the development of a rich soul life in our children today. This tendency is rooted in our concepts of the human being, preconceptions of what a child is, and ideas of what education is supposed to do for our children.

Testing is viewed as a means to determine objectively whether children are actually learning. What it really does is make most children anxious and nervous and unsure of why they are in a school instead of somewhere they can learn about the world that they have to grow into. Children generally do not need testing as it is typically used today, nor do the teachers who must administer the tests. Teachers have their own practical ways of determining progress and learning. Testing is something that governments have devised to make sure nobody learns anything they are not supposed to know, and that nobody learns any more than everybody else does.

Teachers, not necessarily learned educators but real teachers in the classroom, would go an entirely different route from the standard testing route if they had the freedom to exercise their professional judgment and experience. Teachers would simply ask questions, ask for participation and contributions to the class life, and occasionally demand something written. They would present lots and lots of arithmetic problems, with right and wrong answers of course. Watch a master teacher at work with a class; as an observer you would begin to see what the children know and how they express what they know in unique ways.

A school can be like a temple, a holy place where children grow in their capacities, where they acquire the necessary forces of willing, feeling, and thinking to give direction and purpose to their lives. When a school becomes such a place, it is permeated with spirit. A school building does not have to be a modern learning factory—square and cold and lacking in enchantment. After all, it is supposed to enhance the development of children into adults. Why shouldn't the buildings feel human, as though they were constructed for human beings instead of for computers? I am not surprised at the graffiti and the vandalism in some communities. If the buildings were humanized with gentler architectural lines and lovely color and lots of healthy light, becoming places where a human being can feel at home, we might have more respect from children. They would know that we understand who they are and how they strive to be human beings of the highest caliber if only given a chance. Children bring renewed spirit for the conduct of life. When they reach adulthood they naturally find themselves working in either the economic domain of our social life, the governmental domain that maintains our accepted life of rights, or our cultural domain in one of the arts, education, research, religion, or creative leadership.

In our social organism we have three interlocking and collaborative domains that provide balance and counterbalances for the forward motion of human development. The economic domain sustains us all with our worldly needs so that we can exist on Earth in brotherhood and sisterhood. This domain uses our capacities to render this service. It also generates capital through consuming human capacities. The domain of rights ensures that we all have similar opportunities afforded us and that none of us is taken advantage of through our lack or wants. Equality of each and all has to be championed at every step of the way. In itself, this task of ensuring equality is a huge one that we have not fully achieved, even in this country, mostly because our governments are confused and distracted from their main task. The cultural domain renews us, provides the social organism with ever-fresh forces and capacities, and promotes freedom to develop, freedom to serve, and freedom to prosper. It uses up capital in the form of gifts to develop human capacities for the other two domains of our social life.

When we bring consciousness to these three domains, the transactions that occur within them can take on a healing function, because the resources used in each domain are transformed to create change. The movement of money becomes service through the purchasing transaction. The movement of money mediates the equality of rights in all domains and is transformed into renewed capacities in the cultural domain. The seamless integration of three powerful forces in our social life is achieved through the value driven multitude of transactions.

Business translates human energy and capacity into goods and services that meet our needs and support our life on Earth. The spiritual cultural life translates capital into human capacities and renews, in freedom, our thinking, feeling, and willing life forces. Governments and their focus on rights mediate and balance the rights of each individual with the need for equality among all humankind by regulating the healthy movement and speed of money.

Our Social Life: Three in One

The Three integrated, basic domains contained in our social life are 1) the cultural domain, or education, which provides insight and leadership; 2) our life of rights, or government, which ensures equality; and 3) our business domain, which supports all community life with products and services, as well as profit and capital.

When we try to convert the three domains into a picture, we discover that each has a specific gesture. Business has a supportive gesture; education has a gesture of raying into and transformation; government has a leveling gesture. When we draw them they each look somewhat as follows:

Business:

    Supports social life
    Products and services
    Generates profit and capital
    Service motivated
    Promotes brotherhood and sisterhood
    Principal transaction is buying/selling

Education:

    Promotes leadership
    Nurtures human capacities
    Contributes intelligent research and insight
    Instills freedom
    Principal transaction is lending/borrowing

Government:

    Fosters individual rights
    Contributes law and justice
    Regulates the flow of money
    Engenders social conscience
    Nurtures equality
    Princpal transaction is giving/receiving

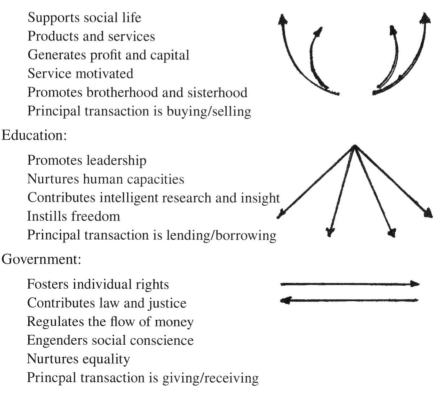

The three basic gestures, integrated into a whole structure, would look like this:

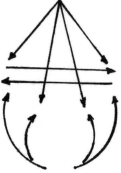

When a number of us gathered in 1981 to change the way the world works with money, we had all these elements in our consciousness as we struggled to find a form that truly corresponded to our highest intentions. We wanted money to move in accordance with the characteristics of the three archetypal transactions. We wanted to explore the kind of consciousness necessary for human beings to take charge of what was happening in our social life and in the life of the Earth. To achieve such a result, we realized we were banking heavily on the capacity for people to change their outlook on money. We felt that humanity was at a new point in development making it possible to change in this way. As we explored the development of human consciousness, we found it was necessary to penetrate human history with imaginative cognition in order to get at the underlying forward motion buried in the wealth of available data. We discovered that the oral traditions in many cultures had more to offer than many of the detailed studies in history texts.

Who are we to think we can develop to the point where we can take responsibility for the Earth? Are we at the beginning or end of our development, or somewhere along the way? How did we mature through eons of time to the current condition of having such thoughts at all? Is there evidence to support the proposition that we are evolving and able to influence what happens next?

In the next section we will consider the evidence of myths, legends, stories, and biographies. We do this because many of us, including myself, see trends that are hard to ignore. Although these records of how earlier humanity viewed its situation are in an imaginary form and come from an oral tradition, they contain wisdom and truth. What do these earlier accounts, handed down through the ages and eventually written down, tell us about the gradual development of what we now know as individuality? We'll begin with the Norse Myths, from a time considered prehistoric; nevertheless, I believe they are truly very early historic information. We will then move on to ancient Greece and to ancient Rome and into later times. With these broad strokes, we will outline the development of the human being from early historic to present times allowing us to identify who in us is able to heal through money.

OUR EVOLVING CONSCIOUSNESS

33. OUR INFANCY

IN OUR DESCRIPTIONS of the three fundamental transactions in our financial life, we recognized that each transaction required two parties. A party to any transaction was described as a legal entity empowered to act as a responsible individual under the law. Who is this so-called individual, and how did individuals come to have rights? Without a reasonable answer to this question, we cannot hope to comprehend the true nature of money.

Science has given us a variety of stories suggesting that we emerged as a matter of natural selection from apes, which in turn evolved from other earlier animal life. Few of us are satisfied with the idea that our precursors were apes. We realize we had a past and that we may have resembled that species, but we are so much more advanced physically, emotionally, and intellectually that it is difficult to feel any real hereditary connection with apes. Instinctively, we sense that a completely new intervention of some kind was needed for us to evolve, not an organic cellular outgrowth. What if an ape can be laboriously taught to distinguish between a piece of paper and a pencil? Does this suggest that the ape could eventually write, say, Tolstoy's *War and Peace?* Something quite dramatic would need to happen to an ape for such a development to occur, even over millions of years.

Fortunately, if we go back in time and read, or decipher, earlier records and writings, we discover that a very different view of our origins dwelled in our ancestors. Their perspective derived from their experience. We can only conjecture from our present perspective about what it was like at that time.

Somewhere along the way, we may have come across the Norse myths or other ancient mythologies, introduced perhaps as an interesting story of fiction. After all, people tell stories all the time. Some have truth in them, while others are sheer fancy. Such invented stories are entertaining but give us little of substance to live by. Mythology is quite different from the typical invented story. To our ancestors, mythology was no different than today's scientific treatise. Myths are handed down from generation to generation. Usually an elder carried the authority to tell a myth to the village, family, or gathering. The elder, in youth, had heard the myth many times before from the elders who learned it from their elders, and then was able to tell it faithfully and with the right inflections and gestures. Thus the chain of mythological story and drama stretched back in time through many generations.

We have no way of knowing how far back in time the myths of the ancient Norse people originated, since they come from a time when writing was not yet an accepted form of record keeping. The Norse people had an oral tradition, and they retained the entire body of their myths in their memories, just a fraction of which is known today, though it fills an entire book. Judging by what has survived in the myths handed down through the ages, our ancient ancestors' ability to remember was outstanding.

Geology, history, and psychology do not give us as clear a picture of the earliest stages of humanity as do the ancient myths of our ancestors. When we read today of some historical event described in a history text, we are served an array of facts, but rarely do we gain any real insight into the causes, underlying trends, and progression of the human drama that took place. Fiction based on historical fact does a better job, though it usually contains interpretation and subjective elements. In the following example of an ancient myth, we find that events are described with a minimum of subjective interpretation. We feel as though we are hearing a matter-of-fact account of exactly what happened and who said and did what. It sounds and feels almost like an eyewitness giving us factual material.

In truth, myths are oral records that depict the way the human beings of their time experienced life. We can accept them just as future generations will accept our written records, emails, and newscast recordings. They may not completely comprehend our narrow perspective and subjective orientation, but they will have to accept the reality of the perspective given in today's scientific papers. They will have to acknowledge that they accurately depict how we regard life and the world.

Following is one story out of Norse mythology, quoted directly from a translation by Dorothy M. Belgrave and Hilda Hart, entitled *Norse Myths*. The names are foreign to us, but we do not always need to know their identity, because the story is self-evident. All we have to do is enter the story with our feelings and experience what is described. The wisdom contained in such myths shines through if we let it.

34. The Doom of Loki
and His Children

IT SEEMED A strange thing that for so many years Odin should have permitted Loki to roam about at pleasure, practicing his harmful devices against both gods and men. Yet in truth Allfather, despite his wisdom, was not allowed by the Fates to know or see everything, and often his hand was held against his will by a power above him, whose omnipotence he felt, yet could not explain.

Whether Loki was blood-brother to the King, born in those far-off times before the giant Ymir's brood had been drowned, whether he was a son of Bergelmer, the only monster who escaped the flood; or whether he was true son of Odin, bred in virtue, but led astray by the Jotuns, no one knew. Yet certain it is, that he would long before have been cast out of the sacred city, had there not existed between him and Allfather a mysterious bond, and had he not so often used his cunning brains to extricate the gods from difficulties into which, as often as not, he had himself led them.

When, however, his love of evil could no longer be ignored—yet before his greater and final crime, the betrayal of Baldur—Odin decided to call a council of all his sons, and seek their advice on this difficult matter.

"Who is there among ye," he said, "that can tell me why Loki is lately grown from mere mischief-maker into downright evildoer? And where does he spend those long absences from his palace, which grieve the heart of his gentle wife Sigyn?" Then Heimdall, whose watchful eye never slumbered, came forward.

"Father, he goes to a wood in Jotunheim, called Jarnvid, and there dwells with the hideous giantess Angurbod, whom, indeed, he has married, notwithstanding his vows to Sigyn. He is at this moment playing with his three monstrous children, while Angurbod watches and encourages them. It is from these creatures that he learns his wickedness."

The gods groaned with horror, as the full perfidy of Loki was made known to them; and Odin at once ascended his air-throne and cast his gaze toward the wood Jarnvid. There, just as Heimdall had said, he saw Loki sporting on the porch of Angurbod's house with three frightful forms, evidently his children. One was like a large and loathsome serpent, yet with a face that bespoke more than a serpent's craft. One was a fierce-fanged wolf. And the last was no other than Hel, whose face and figure could never be described, so terrible were they.

Allfather dispatched his two strongest sons, Thor and Tyr, to fetch up the culprit and his misshapen family, for judgment. At first Loki refused to obey, but soon the threats of Thor frightened his craven heart into submission, and the procession started. The serpent writhed along in front, the wolf leapt from side to side, and Loki led Hel by the hand, while Tyr and Thor marched behind brandishing sword and club. In this order they reached Asgard and followed by all the amazed and horror-stricken gods, made their way to the Great Judgment Hall, where Odin sat waiting. For a few moments Allfather gazed down upon the masters, unable to speak; then in stern tones he addressed the Fire-god, who stood stubborn and defiant before him.

"These then, O Deceiver, are thy foul offspring, and Angurbod it is who has helped thee on thy downward course? No longer may such plagues as these three creatures thrive at large; hear their doom. The serpent shall be cast into the depths of the sea which separates Midgard from Jotunheim; he shall be called Jormungand, the Sea-Snake, and there must he stay buried until the Fates release him. The wolf shall be called Fenris, and he shall be penned in a courtyard on the outskirts of Asgard, fed and looked to by Tyr, who alone is strong enough to control him. Thy daughter Hel, whose hand thou holdest so fondly, shall depart to her appointed place. A throne awaits her in the Underworld, and she shall rule over the kingdom of Death. As for thee, Loki, stripped of these evil children, perchance thy love of evil will lessen, and for the sake of the bond between us, thou shalt keep thy freedom a little longer."

Thus was judgment passed on the children of Loki and Angurbod; Odin's behests were carried out, and for a time all went well. But Fenris grew mightier and fiercer each day, and his cries of hunger before Tyr went to feed him, and his howls of greed as he tore his meat, oppressed all the dwellers in the city, until at length they appealed to their King, saying—

"Allfather, we fear that soon Fenris will grow beyond the control of Tyr, and breaking from his pen will devour us all. Give us therefore a chain with which to bind him.

Odin answered that he had no such chain to bestow, but if they wished they might make one or seek one. At this, Thor readily offered to put Miolnir, his magic hammer, to such good use on his anvil, that an unbreakable chain should be finished by the next morning. And all that night the sounds of hammering proceeded from his smithy, and the sparks flew for miles around, and the bellows blew a hurricane. At dawn Thor emerged black with toil, holding out to the assembled gods the chain Laeding, mightier in each of its links and more virtuous in its metal than anyone could have dreamed. Nevertheless, when they had bound Fenris, neck and foot with it, he merely shook himself and the links tore like paper.

Thor ground his teeth but went back to his smithy and worked again, this time for a day and a night, until he had forged Dromi, which was as strong again as Laeding; and for a second time they bound Fenris, neck and foot. But the wolf only stretched himself, and Dromi fell into as many pieces as Laeding.

The gods went away crestfallen, Thor muttering aloud, "Look not to me for further help. Who is there in the world that can forge more strongly than I?" To which, indeed, there seemed no reply.

Some time passed, and the power and fury of Fenris doubled itself, until Tyr told his brethren that before many more days the beast would certainly break from his pen and wreak mischief in the city. Then Hermod raised his voice.

"Why not send to the King of Dwarfs who lives in Swartheim?" he asked. "Have not the little cave-men fashioned Draupnir, Allfather's wondrous ring? And the ship Skidbladnir, that defies all weather? And Thor's hammer, and endless other marvels? Perchance with their spells they can weave a chain to bind Fenris."

Whereupon the messenger of the Vans, Skrynir, who knew the land of Swartheim, was dispatched with presents and promises to the Dwarf King, and he, when he heard the gods' request, thought for a while with pursed lips and wrinkled brow.

"Yes," he said at length, "it may be done. Wait here for three days and at the end of that time the chain shall be ready."

So Skrynir waited, and on the third day the King put into his hand a soft silken thread, so fine that it could pass through the eye of a needle, and so light in weight that it floated in the air like a piece of fluff.

"You think this will never hold Fenris?" asked the King with a laugh, as he read doubt and surprise on Skrynir's face. "I will tell you what it is made of. It is fashioned out of six things—a cat's footfall, a woman's beard, the roots of a mountain, the sinews of a bear, the breath of a fish, and the spittle of a bird. No strength, however great, can break such a chain, nothing but the sound of the trumpets calling to the Last Battle."

Skrynir now hurried back to Asgard with his treasure, and greatly did the gods marvel as they tried, one by one, and all unsuccessfully, to break or cut the thread. A pleased smile lit up Odin's face as he, with the rest, examined it.

"Go now, my sons," he said, "and if ye succeed in beguiling the wolf to wear this fetter, methinks ye will have no further trouble with him."

But when Fenris saw the delicate thread which the gods had brought, he feared magic, against which he knew his strength was useless. At length he said that he would stand and allow them to wind it about him, if one of them would place a hand within his mouth as a sign of good faith. There was a moment's silence and then Tyr strode forward and calmly placed the whole of his right arm within the cruel hungry jaws. Quickly Thor and the rest wound the thread about the wolf's head, and round his legs, and fastened it firmly to the largest flagstone in the court. Fenris plunged forward, expecting his bond to give like burnt cotton, but the more he struggled, the firmer did he find himself fettered. With an angry snarl he bit off Tyr's hand. He had been beguiled, but he had claimed his hostage.

Loki's three evil children were now safely put into bondage, and there they would remain until the Last Day when both gods and giants should perish. But their father went free, and instead of diminishing in evil, as Odin had hoped, he became less and less like a god, more and more like a devil, until at length, as you know, he committed the greatest treason of all, by betraying Baldur into the power of his daughter Hel.

After that, Allfather could no longer remember the mystic bond which bound him to the Fire-god, and he gave orders that if ever the Deceiver appeared again in Asgard he should be seized and held prisoner. Loki knew full well that his crime against Baldur had won him universal hate, so to escape punishment he fled from the Peacestead on that fatal day, and hid in the mountains; and there he built himself a dwelling with four doors, looking north, south, east and west, and the doors he kept always open. By this means he hoped to be sure of escape if ever the avenging gods should seek and discover him. He planned carefully; that as soon as he should see his foes approaching he would rush out towards the mountain stream which ran down not far from his hut. There he would turn himself into a salmon, and hide among the stones and weeds.

"Nevertheless" he said to himself, "though I could easily escape a rod and a hook, they could catch me if they made a net like that of the Sea-Goddess-Ran."

And this fear so haunted him that he decided to prove whether such a net could be made. One day he was busily at work with his twine and flax when a sudden dart of flame from the hearth made him look up. In the distance, he saw Odin, Thor and many other gods hurrying towards the hut. He sprang up, threw the net into the fire and dashed out towards the stream unperceived, so that when the gods entered they found their enemy gone and nothing but a half-burned net smoldering on the hearth, and some unused twine on the floor.

"What," said one of them, "if he has been testing the power of nets to catch fish? Let us see if the stream yonder be worth dragging."

And they began, with the rest of Loki's twine, to make a net similar to the pieces they saw smoldering. When it was finished they carried it out and cast it into the water, and dragged the stream thoroughly. But Loki, in the form of a salmon, hid between two stones and escaped. A second time they dragged, and now the net was weighted so that it brought stones to the surface. A large salmon came up, leapt high in the air, and dropped into the water.

"'Tis he," shouted Thor. "Once more, brothers, and our enemy will be captured."

Again the net was cast, and this time, as the salmon leapt, Thor caught it by the tail and held it fast, until, almost dead with struggling, it lay faint and still.

"Put on your true form," cried the captor, and the salmon changed to Loki, who sullenly allowed himself to be bound, for he knew that no further fighting could avail him.

The gods then led him down into a cavern in the very bowels of the earth, and there fettered him to three pointed rocks, one for his shoulders, one for his waist, and one for his knees. Over his head, the Giantess Skadi, his ancient foe hung a venomous serpent, from whose mouth fell drops of poison, which burnt and stung like scalding water. Such torment, however, was too terrible even for treacherous Loki, and Sygin, his gentle wife, was allowed to descend to the cavern with a bowl which she held aloft for ever after, catching in it the drops of venom as they fell. Only when she moved to empty the vessel did the drops hiss upon the Deceiver's upturned face, and then he shook the whole earth in his struggles to get free.

Such was the fate of Loki, doomed to lie unpitied, unrelieved, until the Great Day of Doom, Ragnarok, should come. Then he, with his children, and all other evil things, should be loosed from bondage, and the whole Universe should collapse by reason of the mighty struggle between them and the gods. Both sides should perish in conflict, and out of the destruction should arise a new Asgard and Midgard, new forms of the gods, new men and women, fairer and more virtuous than of old. But Loki and the giants, with all their sin and kin, should have vanished forever.[1]

⊷▅▆ ▆▅⊶

There are many interesting aspects to this remarkable story from Norse Mythology. We could easily devote an entire book to fathoming its relationship to other mythological connections and to the meaning of the different segments of this story. You may wish to note some of your own observations and comments and record your insights for future reference.

Human beings are mentioned only twice in this myth—once at the beginning and again at the end. Midgard is the location given for where humans have their lives. On the face of it, this is not a story about human beings at all, except that the reference at the very end suggests humans are deeply affected by what transpires. From our human perspective, the story is about where we came from and what is likely to happen to us in the course of time. The story suggests that what we now know as the human individuality began in the lap of the Gods, so to speak. The individuality in each of us that today is beginning to exert a healing influence on our social life is barely evident in the story and we read nothing of human daily life.

35. WE ARE NOT IMPORTANT ... YET

AS WE HAVE seen this story is about the gods, not really about humans. The various gods are the protagonists, the enemies, the sufferers, the schemers and the winners and losers in conflicts between them. Today the gods are nowhere to be found in our daily lives. Everything that happens is due to some human action or to an action out of what we now call Nature. Just listen or watch any Newscast and you will notice it consists of natural disasters and human events.

When we consider this story about gods and humans we marvel at the difference in our consciousness today. We acknowledge nature, even enjoy it, but where are the "Gods?" They are not readily accessible even to our imagination. That's how far we have come from the perspective of our ancestors who gave us the Norse myths. Our ancient ancestors enjoyed the drama that took place in a spiritual world that dominated their existence. Because their myths are about the gods and not about humans it is clear that they found what the gods did much more intriguing than what was done by their neighbor or even themselves. It must have been awe inspiring to marvel at the actions and counter actions of the gods as they wrestled with the growing presence of evil in their midst. Even today when we read the story of the Doom of Loki, we are struck by the activity of the gods and how they related to one another. With every deed, they shook their universe, as their powers were unleashed.

Are the ideas of evolution and the idea of divine origin incompatible? Are they mutually exclusive? At the core of each of these beliefs is an idea, a concept or several of them. It is only through our thinking that we come up with those two concepts. If we do not acknowledge the validity of our thinking, which in itself is not something visible or material; we must abandon both the concept of divine origin and the concept of evolution. We can't argue the merits of one or the other without first arguing the existence of thinking as a spiritual capacity with which we are endowed.

Without any concepts the world is incomprehensible. It would be a collage of disconnected impressions without meaning because it is only our thinking consciousness that connects it all into a comprehensible whole. The comprehensible whole is the gift of our thinking for which there is no external evidence or proof. We rely on an invisible capacity; namely thinking which is a spiritual activity that gives us our concepts about the nature of the world. Thus we end up with a philosophical catch–22. If we deny the spirit we deny our own thinking. If we base our conclusions on thinking we acknowledge the spirit in us and consequently the spirit in the world.

Once I deny the existence or the validity of this spiritual capacity I must also deny the world conceptions created thereby. Your world conception, my world conception, any of our world conceptions can be traced back to the vitality of our thinking consciousness. I have as much faith in the evolutionary picture of our developing consciousness given us out of mythology, storytelling, and eventually biography as I do in the theoretical descriptions of natural science. That is why I say, our own stories out of an earlier age help us to grasp how we have evolved from children of the gods to individuality.

In this section we begin with an example from the Norse myths because they provide evidence of the consciousness of our ancestors. Our ancestors lived in a world ruled by what they called the gods—spiritual beings who behaved and acted very similarly as human beings do today. We did not consider ourselves important at that time. In short, we were children in the nursery of the gods. By looking at myths and stories in this section we will see how we were created in stages over eons of time, evolving, as do children from babies to adults. Today we are just now at a point in this evolutionary process where it is possible for us to be sufficiently conscious of our responsibility to take charge of our world and ourselves. In order to move money so that it heals human social life; our consciousness needs to penetrate every transaction with soul and spirit.

36. REINCARNATION

NEAR THE END of this story of Loki, in the last paragraph, there is a reference to the collapse of the universe, followed by the rebirth that will come after. Many myths and legends have such ideas built into their very fabric, as if it were understood as a reality. *The Doom of Loki and his Children* from the Norse myths is one story out of many, that suggests we have a limited existence in our present form, but that we re-emerge in the future in a new and better form. That is what is stated in the final paragraph of the written version. We must not forget that all myths come out of an oral tradition spoken by elders within the context of a community. Whatever is written down is simply a recording of what was spoken.

It is said at the end of the story that, like the Phoenix we rise again for a new beginning out of our ending. "And out of the destruction should arise a new Asgard and Midgard, new forms of the gods, new men and women fairer and more virtuous than of old."[2] That's how it is prophesied. How can this be so, unless we continue some kind of existence during the period when we cease to exist? Could it be that in the story of *The Doom of Loki* we have the idea of existence at different levels; a prediction that we apparently disappear from one existence, continue in another form of existence and then re-emerge again in a physical form at a higher stage? Does this story contain a direct reference to reincarnation as a natural process of the individual human being? Does it contain a direct reference to the reincarnation of the whole of humanity and the earth itself our home? Perhaps the individual physical life of our planet mirrors the transformation of the individual human life that takes place through incarnation and reincarnation. In other words, does our planet die and is then reborn in an evolved form?

Is it that human beings reincarnate again and again in stages, owing to the cyclical nature of all life? Just as the sun rises and sets, the seasons move through the year and all plants and animals come and go as part of the natural world, perhaps we humans, each of us a species unto ourselves, come again and again to further develop our full potential. Somehow, this makes sense once we experience the full import of our own inner, spiritual nature and apprehend our individuality as enduring through numerous lifetimes. In other cultures, such as ancient Egyptian, Greek, Indian, and Japanese, and in many religions such as the Hindu and Buddhist precepts, reincarnation was and is an accepted fact.

It seems to me that evolution and divine origin are highly compatible when experienced in the long-term trend from myth to story to biography. Consider the following story out of the *Iliad* by Homer. Notice the different posture concerning the gods and how the human being begins to move more prominently onto the same stage as the gods. The human being is indicated as a player in the world game. This is an example of the evolution from childhood to adolescence. We move forward from prehistoric Scandinavia to ancient Greece and then to ancient Rome, to see what they tell us about our development through the ages. If we delve into these stories, of which many are thousands of years old, we notice a gradual change in the relationships between humans and spiritual beings. If we follow the trend inherent in the actual sequence of these stories it is almost as if we so-called mortals are in a kind of school, an evolutionary school, a developmental school to mature and become what we are today.

The Iliad as told by Homer and later written down is an extended story presented in a book that describes the events that led up to the removal of Helen, wife of Menelaus, King of Sparta, by Paris to Troy. This violation of the rules of honor caused the Trojan War. To avenge the abduction of Helen, the largest armada of Greek ships and warriors the world had ever seen up to that time, followed the two lovers to Troy, camped outside the city, and laid it under siege. Homer describes in minute detail the ten-year battle between the Greeks and the Trojans, culminating in the final story of the Trojan horse leading to the destruction of Troy and the end of the war.

The small section of the *Iliad* I quote here features the fight between Hector, the great warrior of the Trojan army, and Achilles, the great warrior of the Greek army. At the start of this fragment, Achilles has just mortally wounded Hector's brother. Notice how the gods, Athena and Apollo, get involved. (The translation from the Greek is by W. H. D. Rouse.)

37. HECTOR AND ACHILLES

WHEN HECTOR SAW his brother clasping his bowels and sinking to the earth, his eyes grew dim. He could not keep away any longer, but went straight up to Achilles like a flash of fire, balancing his lance. Achilles saw him—sprang to meet him and cried out in defiance, "Near is the man of all others who has struck me to the heart! The man who killed my precious comrade! Now we need not shirk each other along the lanes of battle!

Then he said to Hector frowning: "Come nearer, that you may die quicker!"

Hector answered boldly: "Don't think you will scare me with words, Peleides, as if I were a little child. I can use taunts and abuse myself if I like. I know you are a stronger man than I am, but all that lies on the knees of the gods. If I am the weaker man, yet I may take your life with a cast of my spear, for my blade also has a sharp point!"

He poised and cast his spear. But Athena turned it back from Achilles by a gentle puff of breath, and it fell at Hector's feet. Achilles leaped at him furiously with a shout—Apollo caught him away softly as a god can do and hid him in mist. Thrice Achilles leapt at him—thrice the spear struck a cloud of mist. When for a fourth time he would have struck, he cried out angrily with brutal frankness.

"Again you have just missed death, you cur! That was a nice thing, but again Apollo saved you! Of course you say your prayers to him whenever you go where spears are whizzing. I dare say I shall finish you next time I meet you, if I can find a god of my own to help me. Meanwhile I will try to find somebody else."[3]

The rest of the story of this battle describes the warriors that Achilles kills, how he kills them, and his glorious triumphs.

This story is different from *The Doom of Loki and his Children* because humans now matter and they are the protagonists in the story rather than the gods. Hector and Achilles struggle for honor and glory and fearlessly throw themselves into battles that involve direct physical contact, cutting and smashing and killing each other to prove they are brave and courageous. A man's valor and honor are the main themes in this fragment of the *Iliad*. Yet the humans in the story appear like children because they seem unconscious of their actions which can only lead to suffering and pain both to themselves and to others. Have they no sensitivity or compassion for the human condition? Don't they feel the pain they inflict on each other? It is obvious that they have a different consciousness, one that is imbedded in their own feeling of self so that the other person doesn't yet matter.

True, there would appear to be people today who exhibit a child-like consciousness similar to that shown by Hector and Achilles in the story above. Every time I read a newspaper story of some violent criminal act, I am transported back into an earlier age. There will always be some people at an earlier stage of consciousness and some at a later stage of consciousness. That is because we don't all move forward at the same pace and in the same way. Perhaps all the different stages of consciousness actually exist simultaneously on the face of the earth. However, many times when an earlier consciousness endures for a long time, the new consciousness arrives in a rush, through deep experiences of pain or suffering. For example when I read in the newspapers of Al Gore's suffering from the tragic event around his son's accident and eventually saw the documentary he made, *An Inconvenient Truth*, that was so filled with consciousness about our planet I felt he must have experienced a major change in consciousness. Deep suffering and pain can often bring with them a lift in consciousness.

Another aspect of the story of the *Iliad* from ancient Greece is that the gods are continually mixing into the affairs of human kind. They take sides and they argue among themselves! They bring about natural events to deflect spears thrown by the warriors and stir up mists that hide them from each other. The goddess Athena deflects the spear to protect Achilles. The god Apollo hides Achilles in a mist that protects Hector from the rage of Achilles. Both gods seem to have agendas and strive to protect their favorites.

What we see in Homer's *Iliad* is that there is no doubt that the human being has become important. It is almost as if humans are necessary for the gods to accomplish anything on the earth. Only by influencing human thinking, feeling and willing are the gods able to maintain some control over their actions. Throughout the *Iliad* the gods are continually faced with losing their ability to arrange matters between humans and human families and between the various peoples on the earth. When Helen falls in love with Paris, the gods are forced to deal with the consequences but none of them caused Helen to fall in love. Once Paris and Helen fall in love and determine to escape the authority of Menelaus, Helen's husband, events are set in motion that none of the gods had planned or brought about. When Helen and Paris were in Troy, the gods could only influence one or another of the combatants. This is in contrast to the *Doom of Loki* where the gods were clearly the center of the story and humans just suffered the consequences.

Is this not so with children? Adults always make the decisions, and regardless of whether the adults decide to separate or divorce, the children must learn to live with whatever adults bring about in their lives. *In The Doom of Loki and his Child*ren we are seen as children. In the *Iliad*, we children are beginning to cause havoc, and the gods must suffer the consequences and make the best of it. The gods in the *Iliad* still have control of nature and its forces, but human beings are beginning to escape the dominance of the gods. The gods send mists to hide people in and they deflect spears with a puff of wind. We humans appear to have reached our adolescence and the gods have a hard time with our unruly behavior.

As we move from the *Iliad* of ancient Greece to the stories of ancient Rome, we find new steps in our evolutionary process. In ancient Greece the gods were entangled in human life, but by the time of ancient Rome the gods had withdrawn from human life. They are hidden in temples and can no longer be reached directly by ordinary people. Any individual wanting to make a decision or confronted by a problem or mysterious event in his/her life would consult an Oracle of which there were many at key locations. For example the Oracle of Apollo at Claros is well known to historians and played a significant role in ancient stories.

During the time of ancient Rome, "the law" was also making its appearance as a human creation that could be used to govern human affairs objectively and fairly. Could we, who are so enamored of trends, conclude that human secular life and spiritual life were separating and human beings were becoming more and more estranged from spiritual life and more dependent on our own faculties?

Although money is not specifically mentioned in the section of the story I quote, what we see is that with the gradual separation of the gods from human life, money and law are introduced together. They are connected, as though dealing with money ipso facto requires stronger rules of behavior. Consider, in the next chapter, a story from ancient Roman mythology.

38. THE LAST KING OF ROME

S EVEN KINGS HAVE governed Rome, no more. The first descended from the Gods and when he died became a God. The last king died in shame.[4]

This is the story of that last king, Tarquinius Superbus, as taken from legends passed down by word of mouth from ancient times. I originally wrote this dramatization for sixth grade students in my class, an age on the edge of puberty. It is a good time in a child's life to act out the drama in this story. I have made it as faithful to the original legend as possible.

The sixth king, Servius, was only a slave in the house of Tarquin, which was headed by Tarquinius Superbus. Servius was appointed by Queen Tanaquil because the gods had caused a flaming light to encircle his brow. This was a sign that the gods favored him even though he was just a slave. As long as he was king, Servius was loved by the people and revered for his gentleness and wisdom.

Tarquinius Superbus, who was warlike, cruel, and disrespectful of human life, deposed Servius. His wife drove her chariot over Servius, thus killing him and ending his reign. Upon the death of Servius and after seizing the throne, Tarquinius dismissed the Senate and imposed large taxes to pay for vast conquests on neighboring cities and colonies. Once he was king and supreme ruler in Rome, the people began to suffer. They not only were taxed heavily, but they were frequently thrown into dungeons and even the most powerful citizens began to turn against him.

In the course of time, Tarquinius began to suffer from insomnia and recurring nightmares. He would wake up in the middle of the night, his bedclothes wet with perspiration. Often in his dreams a snake wound its way through his bedchamber hissing "so-o-on." Tarquinius would shout for his guards, but they were never there in time to catch the snake. He began to confuse his dreams with reality and often called the guards many times during the night, expecting the snake might appear. It never did, however, and the guards responded more and more slowly, thinking their king was going mad.

Finally the king called for his sons and charged them to go to the oracle at Delphi and ask the priests of the temple to answer the question, "What means the snake slithering through the king's bed chamber?" The two sons, equally aggressive and cruel, agreed to take their younger brother, Brutus, along for the journey.

At the Delphic oracle, the brothers waited for the priests to emerge. When they appeared in solemn procession and asked the three brothers their purpose in being there, the two eldest brothers stated the question their father requested them to ask. "What means the snake slithering through the king's bed chamber?" The priests conferred briefly and then turned back to the sons.

"Is that really the question you want us to answer?" they inquired.

The two brothers put their heads together, began to argue, and then turned to the priests. "We really want to know which of us will be the next king of Rome."

The priests slowly filed back into the temple and the brothers waited impatiently. The youngest, Brutus, had always been a little backward in his development, and he played patiently with some sticks lying on the ground. In a short while, the priests emerged single file from the temple and their leader stepped forward and addressed the three sons. "He who will first kiss his mother will be the next king of Rome!" said the priests.

Before the priests had a chance to return to the temple and without so much as a thank you, the two older brothers leapt onto their horses and rode off in a cloud of dust, leaving Brutus behind as he kneeled on the ground. The priests observed him silently. Brutus leaned forward and placed his lips against the ground. "The earth is mother to us all," he said.

In time, Tarquinius was deposed by the senate, which had assembled secretly to rebel against the king's cruelty and tax burden. They banished Tarquinius from Rome and allowed him and his family to leave under guard. The Senate decided that no king should ever rule over Rome again and elected Brutus to the office of First Consul. Brutus, in collaboration with the senate, formulated a law declaring that whoever conspires to bring back a king in Rome, shall be put to death without redress.

A few years passed, when suddenly the two sons of Brutus are brought before him and accused with incontrovertible evidence of conspiring to bring Tarquinius back to power. Brutus had the agonizing dilemma of upholding the law that he himself had formulated and losing his own sons, or ignoring the law and keeping his sons alive. Many of the senators argued that his sons would be pardoned and exempted from such a dire punishment; after all, Brutus was First Consul and they were sure everyone would understand.

In a passionate soliloquy, Brutus argued that, if law has any meaning for the governance of human social life, it must be applied equally for every one without exception. If there is no king, the law must be obeyed with equal service and determination. If the law is to replace divine guidance, then it must be obeyed or lose its usefulness.

The story concludes with Brutus ordering the execution of his own sons in order to support the regulation of life through the substance and letter of the law. This story is also a myth that has been handed down in the same way that the story of Romulus and Remus, the two founders of Rome has been passed down as an oral tradition. Romulus was the first king of Rome.[5]

We can observe in this story that the gods could no longer be directly contacted. The gods have retreated into temples and only speak through the priests. We see that in ancient Rome the priests were trained to provide communication between human beings and the gods and only in temples could the gods be consulted by these specially trained individuals. In our time it is the right of any individual to consult his own "muse" or spiritual guide, but in ancient Rome this was hidden from most of the population and only available through the priests who responded to questions and answered in riddles.

It was necessary to know how to ask the right questions in order to get meaningful answers. Is this not the root of our present-day scientific method? Could it be that humanity as a whole was being slowly trained to ask the right questions? We were being asked to employ our wits—our thinking capacity for guiding ourselves through life. This could be why every answer to a question needed to be carefully processed and not just followed blindly. The priests provided a kind of schooling that enticed human beings to develop their intellect for what would become a next stage in human evolution.

We can see that continuing development in the questions of our children. I remember my three-year-old son coming home with a story about something that another child had done and asking the question, "Is what she did good or bad?" As parents we were being relied on to provide the direct answer. At that stage, trying to get our child to think for himself would have been premature. The important thing was to make clear 1) that we knew the difference between good and bad; 2) that it is important whether something is good or bad; 3) that, as adults, we govern our life by what we considered to be good; and finally 4) to give our child a sense that there is a structure in life that honors what is good and avoids what is bad. We were careful to avoid any suggestion that the other child was bad, but only that the action, the deed itself, was bad because it was hurtful and unfair and took advantage of the weakness of another.

My math teacher in the tenth and eleventh grade of high school was a master at enticing us to think for ourselves. He would present us with a problem such as if $a+b=74$, and then ask how many answers are there to this problem. No matter what we said, he would always counter with, "All right, let's work that out and see what we get. Now, how would you go about it?" He knew that thinking needs encouragement and only clear thinking really helps us give guidance and purpose to our lives.

In the same way the priests at the oracle in the Roman story offered little comfort to the three sons. They demanded that they not act as children merely following orders given to them. They were asking the brothers to solve the riddle they presented. The two older sons, blinded by their overbearing ambition took the riddle literally and didn't search for a deeper meaning. Brutus, the youngest son looked for the deeper meaning and acted upon his newfound insight. He had also acquired some wisdom along the way and qualified his ambition to meet his values. After all, it took courage to establish the law in the place of divine guidance. If the gods had not retreated into the temples, we might still be their children! It may also be that we are still in school. The whole of life and the entire material world is a kind of school and they both present us with riddles. In our personal life we are constantly confronted with riddles. Every time we need to assert something or need to decide something we are resolving a riddle.

The three stories, beginning with "The Doom of Loki" from Norse mythology, and then the story from ancient Greece of Hector and

Achilles, and finally the story from ancient Rome of the last king of Rome all depict our schooling from ancient times to the present in a few thousand years. Like children, we gradually outgrew the nursery of the gods, struggled with their challenging riddles and became self-conscious and now self-regulating and creative. Are the gods looking in on us from beyond the sensory world questioning our confusion and nearsightedness, still confident that we will rise to the potential in us for mastering our own souls and eventually the natural world? Has our schooling been successful?

We all live in a stream of time that is created only in the present moment while the future pours in on us and the past shines on in us. When we consider the healing role of money we have to acknowledge a past to be transformed and a future to be kneaded by us into a present in which every transaction becomes a conscious deed. Money can be our great helper as we determine our future and insert our values into the stream of time.

39. THE SCHOOL OF LIFE

Iᴺ "Tʜᴇ Lᴀsᴛ King of Rome," we see that earlier forms of spiritual guidance faded from daily practice and the law was created to take the place of the work previously done by spiritual beings. Does this show a trend in the evolution of human consciousness and give us a clue as to what individuality really is? To act as a self-conscious individual, is historically quite recent. For example, if we look at the period of history known as the Renaissance, we find that artists began to place their names on their work. Doing so was important to the artist and to the art patron in order to know who created the painting, sculpture, or any work of art. It was not enough to place a work of art into existence. The creator had to be proclaimed on the object itself. It had become essential that an object not extruded from nature, but brought into existence through a human individual be characterized as a creation connected to a creator. The much later development of copyrights and patents has been possible due to a solid basis of individuality and individual rights present in the human race.

Before the Renaissance, only kings and aristocrats by virtue of their family and blood relationships were singled out as individuals. With any general rule there are always exceptions, of course. Even in very ancient times, those magical artists who had special powers with which they also endowed their work were known by word of mouth. However even well-known artisans usually did not place any mark on their work that would indicate their rights as creator of the object. The time of the Renaissance could be described as the emergence of the self-conscious creative individuality.

Consider the way in which we contemplate nature; how minute is much of our knowledge of every aspect of nature? This is a more objective stance than if we were immersed in nature with our whole being the way animals, plants, and minerals are. How did we acquire this more objective stance toward nature? Owing to our objectivity to view and know nature analytically, we have separated ourselves from direct involvement. In a way, we could say we have gained a super nature of our own, removed from the direct amalgamation with nature.

Is that the reason we are able to be a knowing being? Is it because we have been lifted a little out of the natural processes that we can have thoughts, ideals and visions for what we wish to accomplish? It appears our need of nature is diminishing and we find it mostly necessary for some nourishment and for medicinal purposes when we sicken. Are we learning to become free beings liberated out of a basic dependence on nature? Are we to insert a new element into the world order? That's what I am learning in this school of the world. We have become free, because only on the ground of freedom can love be generated as our unique contribution to existence.

We can contribute love for all that exists, for minerals, for plants, for animals and for our fellow humans. I have learned that love is not in this world, it is not of this world. Love is something only free human beings can pour into existence. We are love and are just beginning to realize it and by being ourselves more we insert love into existence. Everywhere in nature we can marvel at the wisdom evident within it. Just admire the construction of a beehive. Each chamber in a honeycomb is exactly five sided. This is not independent creativity, it is ordained architecture, wisdom poured into form and activity.

Human beings are also formed wisely. No other form could have permitted us to function as we do. Our arms and legs extend into space ready for sensing and activity. We are unconscious in them, but they follow our determined intentions. Our breathing and heart rhythms connect us with the surrounding world as our breath inhales and exhales us about eighteen times per minute. We actually breathe in and out about 25,920 times in a single day. Resting on our shoulders and riding on us like Humpty Dumpty or a little prince in a carriage is our head, somewhat removed from our bodily functions but still connected, of course. It is in a perfect position to observe, reflect on what is observed, and think. We are indeed fortunate that we are so wisely formed. We are formed to become objective, to become responsible for what we can observe and know, and to develop and unfold the most powerful force ever known in the universe, the power of love.

We will not be able to become truly responsible for our own actions as they relate to other human beings without developing an all-encompassing love for what we are and can become. We need to expand ourselves with love to be responsible for nature and the living earth on which we currently prosper. Love is not just a feeling; it is a transformative force in our souls that can mature and eventually transform the world.

There is a story my mother used to tell me related to this theme. She said the wind blew and boisterously huffed and puffed around the world, challenging the sun with its power. The wind claimed it could have its way with anything in the world, it was so strong. The sun suggested they have a contest to see which of them could more easily take the overcoat off a certain man walking along the road. The wind laughed and agreed. He blew and blew and the more he blew, the tighter the man drew his overcoat around his shoulders. The wind sent his coldest and most violent blast at the man and nearly knocked him off his feet, but the man pulled his coat on even tighter. Then the sun began to shine on the man, giving him all the warmth it could muster. Gradually the man removed his overcoat, his scarf, and his hat. The wind was chagrined but acknowledged the sun as the winner.

This little story compares sheer physical force with the force of something gentler but more effective in the long run. I always thought of the warmth of the sun as being analogous to the force of love which can shine objectively on everything and help it grow and develop. This is the force resident in human souls and powerful enough to transform our monetary system so that it becomes an instrument of love. In so doing we shall without a doubt heal our social life. Our lives are now a kind of school that is teaching us how to employ this transformative force of love in all our relationships.

How can we apply this schooling to the movement of money? Money today is a worldwide system of movement that brings all the results of our labor into circulation and leaves them for consumption wherever they are needed. Money is our copy of the blood and breathing system in our own bodies. It is there to serve us, not to enslave us. Money is ready now to move as we inspire it to move in sync with our developing forces of love for all that exists. Let's at least begin with our sister and brother human beings.

40. FROM GODS TO PRIESTS TO KINGS TO THE LAW TO THE "I AM"

THE SEQUENCE OF stories related here indicates major changes in the form of guidance given to human action. Questions we had regarding what to do when confronted with problems or choices were initially decided for us by the gods as shown in the example of "The Doom of Loki" and similar stories from other cultures. Later, we were directly influenced by the gods but started to become responsible for our own actions and feelings as in the example from the classical Greek culture, the *Iliad*. Then we brought our deepest concerns to the temple, from which our answers came to us in riddles, requiring us to process and think. We sometimes acted naively upon this advice, as children often do, and without fully understanding what it was we faced and its implications for the future, childishly trusting the literal meaning of the directives given us.

You can find the same wisdom in the fairy stories of old for in them you can read similar riddles. Take for example the Russian story of the Little Horse. In one section three brothers set out to find the beast that destroys their father's crops. The older brother usually represents the conservative element. He goes off and is trapped by his own selfishness. The second brother also does not heed the pleas of little creatures like the ants and scoffs at their riddles and needs. Only Ivan, the younger brother, interrupts his quest to help the ants and heed their advice. Why in so many stories is it always the younger, more innocent brother or sister who proves wisest and is successful in the end? Such stories are not myths. They are much newer in origin, but they still contain some of the elder wisdom handed down through the ages as humans extracted themselves first from race, then from tribe, then family and finally achieved autonomy in our modern times.

In the Roman story of the seven kings, the three brothers represented the two forms of consciousness. Two of the brothers took the advice of the priests literally. They accepted in naïve trust exactly what they were told and acted upon it with complete confidence and total lack of understanding. Brutus, on the other hand, represented a further enhancement of our consciousness. He absorbed the deeper elements of the priests' advice, considered his own reality and capacities, and acted courageously out of his own inner understanding of what the words could mean. We see in this story the earlier and the later developed consciousness in juxtaposition. We also see the priests serving the further evolution of humanity. We might say they had a long-term view of the direction in which humanity would evolve and felt it to be their mission to serve as educators, developers of the new, emerging human intelligence.

We also see in this story how the gods were slowly relinquishing the guidance of humanity. Instead of having the temples or oracles available to them, humankind began to form laws to govern their behavior. This story is also about the emergence of law as a purely human invention to regulate what would otherwise be the chaos of our social life. Underpinning all our social activity and supporting it with order and equality is our network of laws and commonly accepted codes of conduct. We sometimes complain about the cumbersome bureaucracy of much of our judicial system, but it must not be forgotten that we ourselves created it probably with very little direction from above or any sources outside of ourselves. In some ways it is one of our greatest achievements. As is always the case, necessity provided considerable motivation.

The story also shows us the anguish of a modern human being forced to face the imperfections of the law and the recognition that there is nothing better available at this stage of evolution. It may be imperfect, but without it we are lost. We created the law and we uphold it by sacrificing some of our willfulness. We give up being a law unto ourselves for the sake of an orderly social life in which every human being has an objectively equal right to exist. Put somewhat differently, the law requires a further development or socialization of humans for it to work. What we created demanded that we consider the welfare of others, of the community as a whole and that we act in such a way that certain rights are afforded equally to all human beings.

Think of a person exercising the right to free speech under the window of a person living in the city on the first floor. While one is exercising free speech, the person forced to listen wants the right to privacy. Sidney Hook, professor of law at New York University loved to pose such situations and force his students to argue both sides of the issue. His point, of course, was that every right, when exercised without consciousness of others, infringes on one of the rights of another.

With the law, we have a stage of further development in which individuals willingly subjugate themselves to the common good. Whereas in earlier times we had strong families and clans, with today's law we have the possibility of common human good available to all, withheld from none. That this potential has not yet been fully realized is to our shame, but does not detract from the fact that it is possible. Human law provides individuals with rights and gives humanity as a whole a sphere of equality, which gradually developed until the French Revolution brought it thunderously into our awakening consciousness in the late eighteenth century. Appropriately the motto of the French Revolution was Liberty, Equality, and Brotherhood.

Who knows what forces drove the French Revolution in the direction it took? Certain ideals surfaced in humanity and rocked the existing social structures of the day. In a society ruled by kings and the nobility, which had come to behave outrageously, the people began to awake to their innate rights as human beings. The fact that freedom belongs only in the cultural domain, equality in the role of governments, and brotherhood made sense only in the economic domain had not yet become a conscious fact. It is only just beginning to reveal itself and of course our founding fathers, when they established the three branches of our government had a sense for this threefolding of social life. The congress, executive and judicial branches are modeled around an instinctive feeling of the archetypal threefolding of our social life.

In all of our natural attributes and gifts we are unequal, different from each other. In all our spiritual and soul constitutions we are differentiated and unequal. However, with the creation of the law and a realm of rights we have established a purely human plane in which each human being regardless of all differences in other domains has equal rights with every other. We managed to create a purely social, non-spatial domain in which equality of all humanity is honored. That domain exists only to the extent and as long as we will it to be. Like music, it exists only while it is being created and passes away when the human activity that brings it about stops.

Imagine you are listening to a Mozart symphony or an opera such as the *Magic Flute*. When the last chord of the orchestra finishes and fades into silence, and just before the thunderous applause begins, you still hear the sound with an inner ear, as though it is resonating in you. Even that fades, however, and Mozart's symphony is no more. The fact that it is written down in sheet music means only that it can be recreated. This is why we and only we, out of our newborn individuality, continuously sculpt a social realm visible only to those with the imagination and perception to create it and feel it and see it. We call it the law. However, it is even more than that. It is the assurance that our contemporaries legitimately recognize us as individuals with rights.

The law is in a realm above nature, where it exists as long as we will it to exist. By that I mean it is not a stone, nor is it a plant, or an animal. It is none of the natural phenomena in our experience and it does not present itself as an objective entity. It is a fabricated realm that we maintain and develop voluntarily to meet our growing consciousness. It is also not a material entity and does not exist in the physical, material world. It is a soul construct that exists only in our consciousness and finds its validation in a variety of written rules, precedence, papers, and books that we create and sustain with our behaviors.

The law, our human rights, and economic values that circulate the globe and carry the flow of money with it, all exist in the same realm. What humankind today recognizes as individuality within the context of self-imposed lawfulness emerged from a time when humans were guided and determined by spiritual beings. It then progressed to a stage that involved being more closely ordered and regulated through the influence of priests and priestesses specially trained to commune with "muses," or as they termed them, the gods. Finally, we have our modern condition of facing the whole of life without much outer guidance, weakening traditions and only gradually strengthening inner resources to turn the tide from lonely independence to growing responsibility for the whole of humanity and the world our earthly home. Into this world we injected the circulatory monetary system as a means for instilling into it our highest values. The fact that the full range of all our values is not yet fully in evidence is simply because we are still developing.

Every time we buy or sell, we affect the entire earth. The whole world is energized by our transaction and is stimulated to produce another product just like the one we purchased. Every time we lend someone money or borrow, we tighten the bonds of community and stir karmic connections in one another. Whenever we give, we insert dearly held values into the climate of our social life. We, the people of today, are taking hold of our worldwide financial circulatory system and are beginning to augment the wisdom-filled world of our senses with the forces of our love. This is the beginning, the very early beginning, of a trend that will stretch as far into the future as it took the universe to bring us to today.

We looked at myths, stories, and history to discover some long-term trends in the evolution of humanity. To understand more fully what it is to be a responsible individual within the context of our own lawful structure is an essential requirement necessary to engage in any of the financial transactions we take for granted today.

Moving money, which is what we do in every transaction, is a social act between responsible individuals that affects the social climate and shapes our future. To the extent that we are conscious, every transaction has deeper implications. Every transaction defines us as individuals but also determines how we develop our consciousness further. Can we imagine a time when we carry in our awareness an all-encompassing knowledge of the manufacturer, the product's design and efficacy, how the workers are treated, and what the effect is on our natural world before we buy? Can we imagine a time when ethical buying becomes natural for us and that we wouldn't dream of purchasing something we know works harmfully against our common good? Then we will no longer ask for "what I need." We'll ask for "what I need that will also stimulate sustainable progress for humankind." Ethical individualism will then become the common view. It will be a time when the law gradually dissolves into a framework of individualized decision making, not at odds with any acceptable law, but stemming out of the mature individual as a free deed rendered on behalf of and for the good of the entire community.

The law is fundamentally a restrainer, not a prescriber. The law does not dictate what the individual should do; it identifies unacceptable behavior and determines appropriate punishment for transgressors. As stated previously, the law does not ensure a person's right; it determines only the remedies for an infringement once an individual is charged and found guilty. As an example, the movie *Lethal Weapon* tells the story of an individual who intuits or learns of an event that is about to happen. The police are helpless and can do very little to prevent a crime. They must wait for the crime to happen, and then they can act to find the transgressor; thus the law is generally most effective when it comes to punishing transgressors.

Ethical individualism requires the further development of the individual. It is more than a conscience; it also respects what flows out of individuality as initiative for the good of all. As each individual person evolves to a purer individuality the laws will become internalized and brought alive as living awareness of what humanity requires for its further development. Are we talking about utopia or a world composed exclusively of "good" people who are virtuous and selfless? Absolutely not! The challenges will always be present. Being alive means living in a world subject to pressures that hinder us or help us. Will we ever not be subject to temptation? Will it not be tempting to win an advantage at the expense of another? The temptation will always be there. It's when we are aware of what is least in us that we gain the freedom to develop what is great in us. Good is possible only within a total context in which evil also has a right to exist. The challenges may even grow in scope and intensity. As the good in us develops, evil will likewise flourish. By "evil" I mean only such acts or influences as work against the further evolution of the human individuality and the flowering of the best in the human soul.[6]

41. WHO ARE WE?

WHEN I STAND before you, as an individual human being, you perceive all the details of my appearance. This includes also the way I stand, move my arms, the expressions on my face and even the details of my hair or the lack of it, wrinkles in my face, or a mole or old scar down one cheek are observable with the senses. All of this cannot be hidden from you. You see it all and notice it while I stand before you. There is the sound of my voice, its pitch, and its timbre. You also notice the inflections of my voice, what I emphasize and what I don't. You see the gestures I use to bring across my meaning. You also notice how I change color when I get excited about some topic I am describing.

Anything you can perceive about me through your senses, and this is true of any of us, is actually very, very old. All scientists agree that the human physical body was not fashioned in a day or two. It took eons of time to selectively draw the human form out of inorganic matter, out of plant existence, out of animal existence and finally out of lower human forms. What you experience of me with your senses is ancient. What we all experience of each other through our senses is ancient. What you see of me is as old as the universe itself. I walk around in an antique body as my sole basis for perceiving and expressing myself!

What you don't see and what you can't experience with your senses is *me*. I, in this ancient body, invisible to the outer world, am a recently arrived child of the universe, wanting to be recognized and comprehended. All of us human individuals long to be recognized. Our first experience of a spiritual being should be to recognize one of our own, one another. The process for recognizing the individuality striving to become active in another human also requires imaginative cognition or active thinking. How else are we to "see" what is invisible? We are able to see in the same way the artist sees with his soul and his heart the painting he longs to reveal on canvas. His act of creativity brings the invisible into the visible. It brings what is spiritual into what is material.

The stages of development depicting our spiritual birthing process through Norse mythology, ancient Greece, ancient Rome, and the
Renaissance is the story of our divine individuality separating itself
from the world divine which intentionally separates from us so that
we can begin to assume responsibility for all that once was carried by
the divine.

Individuality is the world divine lighting up from within the human
being. It is our chance to validate the course of history and process of
evolution, which has brought us to the present age in which the creative
forces that made us have completed their withdrawal and are betting
on our further development. We could say that today the human being
is at the center of the known universe and that the entire future is in
our hands. Once upon a time we were at the periphery. Now we are
the center and we have been given and have taken our freedom to be
the central protagonist in this continuing story of human evolution.
Individuality, the god within each of us, for better or for worse will
determine how we progress further in our evolution. Can we meet the
challenge of our full potential?

Individuality may first appear as selfishness but that is only a phase.
Selfishness feeds upon itself and overcomes itself and progresses
toward altruism. Recently we have seen the remarkable generosity of
several dozen wealthy and famous individuals who came to realize
their potential for good. They were not only listed in a double issue
of *Newsweek,* June 10, 2006, but were described in detail over some
thrity-two pages. What they cared about, how they went about giving
their time and money, and their reasons for being benefactors is thrilling to read.

Individuality and money are inextricably intertwined. I could also
use the ancient proverb "Spirit is never without matter. Matter is never
without Spirit" and translate it for our use into "Individuality needs
money to express itself. Money moves only under the influence of
human intentions." Money is the medium for the spirit in humanity
to transform our civilization and to humanize it in accordance with
our deepest intentions. We have understood that money does not move
through physical force, but entirely through the social forces inherent
in every transaction.

Our present situation is one in which many of us have the inner freedom to determine our own purpose and direction in life. We realize that

every action we take either furthers or hinders our progress. To move money so that it heals requires us to be awake in every transaction. That is the chief reason why a number of us gathered as early as 1981 to explore the spiritual significance of money and to consider establishing a responsible legal entity to serve the many people desiring their money to serve the social aims of humanity. Out of this early study together we eventually created RSF (Rudolf Steiner Foundation) which is described in the next section, as an example of the many remarkable organizations sprouting up in a spring of social renewal all over this country.

The Example of RSF

42. Spirit and Money Matter

THE MESSAGE IN the first six sections of this book is that money has metamorphosed over time as the human being developed. Included is the idea that karma plays into all financial transactions, even though institutionalized banking hides this influence to some extent. Also expressed is the thesis that the spirit, or individuality, in each human being is gradually taking on responsibility for human social life and the management of the natural world. How we work with money has a direct relationship to this growing responsibility emerging in every human soul. It is the call of our time to respond to this need for human self-management, social and world management.

The story of the Rudolf Steiner Foundation (RSF) demonstrates in real time the organizational birth, growth, transformation of forms, influences of spiritual forces, and the determination to change how the world works with money. It models how individuals and organizations change and develop in response to the growing need for conscious awakening to the soul and spirit at work in all events social and natural. RSF is an example of how the economic, rights and cultural domains of our social life reveal themselves through the worldwide circulatory movement of money. It was created to act as an agent of change in how we view money and how we relate to it through our deeds. In this respect, the story of RSF is an example for study so that we all can grow wiser from its practices and discoveries. RSF demonstrates that karma matters, that spiritual insight leads to inspiration, and that the world changes only when humans are imbued with the presence of spiritual forces.

In the beginning only a few people assembled to form RSF. They knew each other, but had never worked together on the same social impulse. I briefly describe each of them below because each of their biographies is a fitting preparation for the initiative they were about to undertake.

John Alexandra had been a teacher and leader in the Green Meadow Waldorf School in Spring Valley, New York. He was taking his CPA exam while we formed RSF and then took a Controller position at Morgan Guarantee. He was wise and fearless in the manner in which he faced the challenges of the school and subsequently the challenges of RSF. His intelligence was free ranging and he was both a realist and an idealist. John was always willing to serve a greater good and did not place himself into the foreground but rather at every step offered his service. During the first months he said to me, "This is your initiative! I take responsibility to actively help you bring it about." His support and his sacrifices made it all possible. Through his vision and skill we ended up with an accounting system that reflected our ideals and responded to every transaction so that reporting, billing, and fund statements were consistent with our intentions.

Mark Finser was the youngest of the volunteers and clearly stood for the future. His involvement meant that the forces of the future would be present in all our deliberations. He brought incredible relationships with people to the table. His experience in social services— working in a community for disadvantaged and socially handicapped young adults—had given him as many as forty employees to supervise and build into a team, even though he was the youngest among them at age twenty-three. He also brought strong envisioning capacities to the group giving birth to RSF. Mark was always ready to consider additional options. He listened to all that was being said and the ideals being expressed and recognized in them his purpose in life. It wasn't long before he was volunteering his services. He was remarkably skilled in bridging between young and old, between those familiar with RSF and those who were not. Repeatedly, Mark connected people to each other and found the common ground for all to participate. Eventually he became the first employee and rapidly took on a position of leadership.

When he eventually became President of RSF in 1997, Mark worked to make RSF into a financial services organization that would carry a spiritual impulse deeply into the material world. He wanted it to model a way that future generations can relate to one another in every transaction. He brought a cosmopolitan viewpoint into all the work and began his unique approach, knitting together striving individuals into a socially renewing fabric.

Ann Stahl was a kindergarten teacher at Green Meadow Waldorf School. She brought an element of soul and warmth into every contact and transaction. Her special work with young children enabled her to value ritual, love the simple things in life, perceive meaning in every detail, and encourage warmth for the human possibility in each of us. Ann's unique way of taking in the smallest detail during a client visit brought out RSF's special way of dealing with client information. She not only observed every detail, she actually participated quickly in whatever was going on, from setting up the meeting room to helping clear up after the meeting. She was a woman of action who observed well while active.

As for me, I had been a teacher at the Rudolf Steiner School in New York City and was exposed to that school's venerable leaders, worked under their tutelage and absorbed their relationships and ways of working together. I eventually left the school, which took me into Barrington & Company, a consulting firm in New York City. Soon I managed a human resource section of the firm and then found myself being sought by Xerox Corporation to run a division specializing in educational contracts with the government. Eventually, ITT recruited me to form a department dealing with executive development in its world headquarters where the new field of organizational development was being learned and implemented in a unique way. I was promoted to serve in Brussels, Belgium, to spearhead the development of executive strength in an international environment. My responsibilities extended over Europe, Africa, and the Middle East. I was then promoted to head ITT Executive Development worldwide at the ITT World Headquarters in New York City. In my spare time I was president of the Threefold Educational Foundation in Spring Valley, New York, and treasurer of the Anthroposophical Society in America, with headquarters in New York City.[1]

Very soon, another important member joined this group of four individuals. Philip Mees was a banker—really the only one of us who had extensive experience in banking. He took it upon himself to make sure all the thinking was clear and accurate. Many a time during decision-making involving a possible loan, he pulled out his pencil and a pad and started with, "Now let me see if I have this correctly." By the time he finished his process, there was a high probability that the analysis would end up with clarity. He also brought great supportive human warmth and interest to the often-methodical grunt work behind the scenes. Eventually he retired from Manufacturers Hanover Trust and served in a variety of leadership functions for RSF over the next fifteen years.

Shortly thereafter and in connection with the very first socially constructive project, Dominic DiSalvo joined the group as a trustee. He was a Boston based businessperson who had sold his business and began a remarkable fifteen years of volunteer service to RSF and its clients. He brought to the work a clear head that never wandered far from the essentials. For many people the "bottom line" left them mired in the material world. Dominic had a knack for finding the core of a problem or opportunity without losing his full humanity and anchoring his suggestions and conclusions in spiritual insight. He was always treasured by the clients and frequently visited them at crucial moments in their development.

These six individuals assembled for the beginnings of RSF and contributed immense gifts and capacities to its formation and service. This organization never would have come about had the choreography of the world not assembled this exact configuration of humans on its behalf. Except for Ann Stahl and Dominic DiSalvo, all of them started their lives in Europe. Mark Finser was actually conceived on the ocean liner between Europe and America, but was born in Switzerland, the rugged and beautiful land of bankers and independent souls. His first birthday took place in the United States. I was born in Europe, but by the time of my third birthday I was in the United States. John Alexandra had all of his early education in Europe before coming to the United States. This group bridged and blended the cultural richness of Europe with the vitality of America.

Half of us were entirely or partially educated in Waldorf schools, and except for Mark Finser, all of us were in the middle years of life. Moreover, all of us were men except Ann Stahl. Whenever the word *except* enters a situation, it demonstrates that creative life is at work. Life does not operate like a machine; it is more a creative process than an engineered device. That is why present science stops at the threshold before life. Materialists manage well the comprehension of all that is mechanical but when they confront life they are at a loss. The creative forces in all that is living, even in human organizations and structures, move in rhythms and always include "exceptions." The "except" in the midst of this group demonstrated that life was at work.

They were all, without exception, students of Rudolf Steiner and operated out of the world conception and threefold view of the human being and social life, which is mentioned in earlier sections. All had participated in study groups, most had leading roles in the Waldorf school movement, and all were active in some form of meditative practice.

Did this group form RSF or did it bring this group together? We are accustomed to having our effects come after their causes. In the material world this certainly seems true. Whenever we notice that something is an effect, we look for the cause to be either simultaneous or in a prior time. We never observe effects and then look for their causes sometime later. How can effects possibly stem from causes that follow them?

RSF as a legal, social organism became visible and active in its present form in 1984. As a spiritual reality, however, RSF may have been the architect and mover of the choreography that brought just the right six people together at the moment in time and place when it could begin to manifest. The spiritual RSF was seeking its moment of birth and gathered six midwives out of the stream of time. The karma of these individualities, how their lives had prepared them for this task, how they related to one another, and how their imaginations were inspired by the spiritual RSF, models the way that spirit intertwines with human intentions. How we actually came together will be described shortly.

In the very beginning, all the founding members were volunteers. Mark Finser was the first employee, followed six months later by Ann Stahl. They both were employees but also volunteers, as RSF could manage only very modest compensation. Philip Mees became an employee when he took early retirement from Manufacturers Hanover, again at very modest levels of compensation. John Alexandra, Dominic DiSalvo, and I remained volunteers and never took employment with RSF. Recently, RSF has contracted with me to provide advisory services to some of the clients. None of the employees in the early years were motivated by ambitions for wealth or power or prestige. All were filled with excitement for the difference RSF might make in how the world works with money.

How instructive it would be if the leadership of organizations would occasionally review their birthing process to uncover its mysteries. It could be an exercise of renewal for an organization to review its biography in connection with the individual biographies of its leaders. Such work would reveal the spirit in the organism and lead to a renewal of intentions and energize the employees. Another useful exercise for an organization is to investigate the time prior to its beginning, tracing the paths of its founders, noting how, why and when they met, and trying to discover in the individual biographies the effects of the spiritual organization they were eventually to found. In this way leaders would discover the origins of their inspirations are present long before they reach consciousness. Long before any of these six people assembled to form the RSF, various events in their lives were preparing them.

RSF was originally incorporated in 1934 and meandered for fifty years, fulfilling only modest purposes. Behind the scenes, however, the spiritual RSF was busy arranging biographical situations that would eventually lead to its rebirth. In 1984 the people and the cultural climate was ready. It was reborn in 1984 and launched into its renewed life with incredible inner energy and became the legal and social RSF. The six servants who were responsible for the renewal of the organization alternated between making things happen and feeling that we were being blown along by an invisible force. This made us all conscious on a daily basis that the growth of RSF was a material unfolding of the creativity inherent in the spiritual RSF. Spirit and matter were joined in the RSF. You will notice this feature as I describe the actual events leading up to the re-founding in 1984.

In addition to the actual founders of RSF I would like to pay tribute to a few of the dozens of human beings who gave of their time and energy in the early years of RSF as members of the Board of Trustees. In the first years, between 1983 and 1988, they included Dietrich Asten, Henry Barnes, Herbert Fill, Edward Leskowicz, Jorge Sanz-Cordona, Manfred Maier, Werner Glas, and Traute Page.

At a time when the RSF experienced significant defining moments in its young life, Dr. Cloppper Almon, economist and professor at the University of Maryland, served as a trustee and was particularly courageous and helpful with his clear thinking and strong heart forces.

I am grateful to all of those mentioned and the many, many not mentioned who contributed to the growth and development of RSF.

43. PREPARATION

IN 1979, as treasurer of the Anthroposophical Society I was involved in extending an invitation to three amazing individuals to tour this country, visit seven key locations, and give lectures about money and banking. All three were intimately involved as pioneers in establishing the Gemeinschafts Bank in Bochum, Germany, a bank experimenting in new forms of community creditability for loans and achieving socially sustainable projects.

The Gemeinschafts Bank had loaned 1,000 Deutsche Marks to each of 200 families that were customers of a biodynamic farm. The biodynamic approach includes the organic approach but adds a spiritual component and redefines the relationship of the farm family to the land defining farming as a profession rather than as a business. The 200 customers in turn gave the amount of their loan, 1000 DM into the farm account to support its operating budget for one year. Each customer signed a promissory note for 1,000 DM and paid it back over the next twelve months and became a member of the farm community, receiving a share of its products at no additional cost. Many participated in projects or workdays on the farm as well. Whether the amount of food exactly equaled the 1000 DM was beside the point. What mattered was that 200 people in community around a farm found it important to sustain its existence for the sake of good food and a healthy environment. It was the forerunner of what we today call Community Supported Agriculture (CSA).

The inspirational leader behind the creation of this bank was a man by the name of Ernst Barkoff, a lawyer with deep interest in saving the environment for humanity and in creating community around financial structures. His two compatriots, Rolf Kerler and Gisela Reuter were equally inspiring and dedicated human beings. As treasurer of the Anthroposophical Society in America, I was keen on hearing more of their approaches to money and to social renewal around farm projects. With the support of the society's executive committee, the three founders of this unique bank were invited to lecture at seven key locations in this country and to share their ideas.

The first lecture was to be given in Spring Valley, New York, in the beautiful auditorium of the Threefold Educational Foundation. They arrived the day before the first lecture to settle in and become acclimated to the new time and culture. As we welcomed them and chatted socially, it became quite clear that they did not speak English. Of course, all educated Europeans speak some English, but it would have been impossible for Ernst Barkoff to deliver his lecture in English. He turned to me and asked if I would translate for him. He was charming and entirely trusting, even without knowing me. Can you imagine—I answered yes! He immediately relaxed and went about his business in complete confidence that the matter had been settled.

I on the other hand was appalled at what I had done. The minute the word slipped out of me I went into shock. My mother sometimes spoke German with me, but I always answered in English. I grew up in this country, had all my schooling in the United States, and took a little German in High School and in College, but not enough to be a translator. Oh well, I thought, I'll muddle through and do the best I can, thinking of the little bit of ordinary daily German that I was familiar with. When it was time for the lecture, Earnst asked me to come up and stand on the stage with him. We waited briefly for silence. I looked around and suddenly realized that about half the audience knew German and would be checking every word I translated.

Ernst Barkoff was a powerful speaker. Magnificent concepts rolled off his tongue mesmerizing the audience even those who did not understand a word of what he was saying. After just one long, German type sentence, where you wait an eternity for the verb that explained what was happening, I thought he would stop while I puzzled over what he had said. But no, he went on to complete his first round of earth-shaking thoughts. I was paralyzed. Fear gripped my insides. I was so darned visible up on the stage. For a moment I thought I should just apologize, ask for another volunteer translator, and slink off the stage. My fear was so great that I couldn't even bring myself to do that. Instead, something quite remarkable happened.

All at once, I turned into a kind of sponge. My ego disappeared, all my defenses evaporated, and I stood there like a small child and soaked up all his marvelous ideas, without any filters or translation occurring.

After about three, or maybe even four minutes, Ernst stopped and turned to me for the translation. I opened my mouth and spoke freely in English out of what he had poured into me and I had soaked up. Nobody in the audience laughed. They seemed to make sense of what I said in English. I was encouraged to go on and finish in this same way a lecture that finally ended about seventy-five minutes later. The two of us shared the applause, and he was very gracious.

I translated for him at a few other locations. He later told me that I had actually transformed the essence of what he had to say into the English idiom and co-created his lectures together with him. This profound way of translating opened up to me a brand new way of listening to my fellow human beings and to the sounds of the world. Now, when a cardinal exposes his nature from the very top branches of a tall tree, I hear not just the sound, but also the cardinal's nature expressing itself in the only way it knows, and I rejoice.

When anyone speaks to me now, I hear the words, the sound of the voice and the feeling living in the thought being expressed. More than anything else, however, I hear with my inner receptivity the being of that person struggling with the real communication of the soul. The real communication is never at odds with the words, the ideas, and the feeling expressed; it is just another dimension of understanding that calls out to me. This I learned from translating the late Ernst Barkoff. To this day I owe him a great deal for having had the privilege of transforming his great thoughts into English.

An additional benefit of translating Ernst Barkoff, which I barely realized at the time, was that soaking up all his magnificent ideas in such an unfiltered, defenseless manner, I had in me a treasure to call on in the years to come. On the last day of his visit we were in the car together on the way to New York City for a last meeting. John Alexandra, who would later be a key person in re-founding RSF, was also with us in the car. Ernst turned to us in the back seat and asked when we were going to start a bank in this country like the Gemeinschafts Bank. We were surprised, but not unpleasantly so, and cautiously admitted that we would think about it and see what we could do. Ernst then promised that whatever we needed, he and his bank would respond with trust and confidence in us. He seemed to be saying that we were members of his trusted karmic family, which I am sure we were.

John Alexandra and I began to meet for breakfast once a week in a basement restaurant in downtown New York City, in the financial district. The restaurant was called Hamburger Heaven. I'm not sure what to say about the appropriateness of the name, but it served us well. We began to struggle with what we saw as the need to bring spiritual understanding and spiritual impulses into the movement of money. We also saw the difficulties and realized that dealing with money was a little bit like trying to pick a rose out of a thorn bush. Nevertheless our earliest concepts were ironed out in Hamburger Heaven early in the morning before the business day opened up on Wall Street and the hordes of financially acute humans poured out of the subways and through the streets to disappear into the skyscrapers of downtown New York City.

We met sometimes at our homes in the evening, struggling to understand the nature of money. Mark Finser was drawn into the project in an interesting way. He had been visiting in Indiana when he needed an operation and rushed to a hospital near our home where he discovered that his employer had absconded with the health insurance money leaving him without coverage. This led him, quite independently to be concerned about money and health insurance and interested in changing the manner in which employees and employers interact over such issues as money and health insurance.

That is how he happened to be in our home recovering from his operation while these discussions were taking place. He connected his own concerns over money and health insurance with the entity that appeared to be forming. Mark's job required supervising a number of social workers and attendants in a community for emotionally challenged teens. He was a good manager and adept at involving others around issues. As a volunteer, he started to get involved with the ideas of RSF, took a definite interest, and became part of the founding group of RSF. Eventually he came along on our first site visit with a potential client and was hooked.

We explored putting some ideas onto paper in a kind of crude brochure but we didn't like the first and tried for several more versions. John Alexandra was using a word processor on a computer in the office of the Threefold Educational Foundation. He threw away, into the wastebasket the first version and worked on another. Ann Stahl, who was a kindergarten teacher at Green Meadow Waldorf School, was very interested in recycling paper whenever she could. In passing the wastepaper basket near where John was working, she picked out the discarded first draft of the RSF brochure, looked at it, and asked John what it was. That's how Ann became involved. I describe this level of detail to show how the choreography played out, how the key people were drawn in through a variety of accidental events and coincidences. Mark through the fact that he happened to be recovering from his operation in the house where RSF was shaping itself. Ann by happening to be in the office where the brochure was being created, happening to look into the wastebasket and happening to see John there and asking, "What's this?"

One evening in Harlemville, New York, I attended a concert given by a very talented woman playing Chopin's music. She played wonderfully and was very much appreciated. That evening, I was introduced to Philip Mees, the pianist's husband. Strange, isn't it, that he happened to be a banker, a VP at Manufacturers Hanover Trust? Philip had been in a study group discussing Rudolf Steiner's ideas on the world's economy and money for years. He had become frustrated because the study did not lead to practical applications of some sort. When he heard about the beginnings of RSF he felt that this was a chance to bring Steiner's ideas into practice. Accidental, unplanned occurrences like that were happening right and left. We talked and you see our founding group was forming itself out of the intricate choreography of the world that inevitably brings together the right people for important initiatives.

44. THE INSPIRATION

THE FOUNDING GROUP met for a year in the financial district in New York City, sometimes in one of our various offices and many times over the phone. We were hammering out the basic intentions. We wanted clarity in how to proceed and were searching for the right language to express these intentions. Very soon it became clear that the ultimate purpose was to change how the world views money and to change how we work with money. For all of its obvious characteristics, the real identity and potential for the future of money seemed illusive.

There is something almost swashbuckling and irresponsible in how money is dealt with in society at large. All kinds of hypotheses abound on how to make money, how to spend it judiciously to get the best deal, and how to put it to work. At the time we were meeting money was being considered as a kind of work force in the economy, and there was no doubt that RSF as a laboring entity was undergoing its own division of labor.

At one point in one of our many meetings, a remarkable woman joined us and, without first asking what we really imagined for ourselves, she proceeded to describe her business, which speculated in currency shifts around the world. She made it look like we could make millions in no time at all. We looked at each other and thanked her for the presentation. It made one thing clear. We were not interested in joining that throng—the throng that milks the economies of the world for private benefit. We clarified for ourselves that fees and income were required to survive and accomplish goals, but they would never become the motive. The motive would remain, for all time, to render service to those human beings of any religious, scientific, or artistic persuasion who were initiators of activity that benefited the advance of the human spirit.

In the larger context of the world very little concern existed for the question of what money is. Everyone uses it daily and is consumed with the idea of making more of it. It is assumed that everyone knows what money is and, further, that they don't need to know more about it as long as they know how to handle it, make it, and spend it wisely. I once had the opportunity to lead a discussion within a seminar for loan officers of a bank. I asked them to describe what they thought money was and how it really contributes to our life. There was some embarrassment and then a number of jokes. The gist of the contributions over which everyone laughed, involved comments like "if you don't know by now, you don't belong in this business," or "show me your money and I'll recognize what to do with it," or similar jibes. Then one loan officer said he had been approached by his son, attending college and asked how he could be in such a greedy business. The others paused and then began a most interesting discussion on the values of young people and how they so often despise what their fathers do for a living and yet take full advantage of all the benefits they receive. I remember then thinking a new generation is coming into the world with deeper intentions toward our social life than the one generally held by my generation. Thus it has become. Most of our clients are younger than I am and are visibly determined to change how the world currently views money.

In the meantime, the founding group at RSF struggled with texts of Rudolf Steiner's lectures, *World Economy,* with many questions: What is capital, really? When did it arise in history, and why is it burgeoning in our economy? What is interest, and how should we all work with it? What is the role of money in human society, and why are we not satisfied with its current, apparent power? We gradually concluded that we wanted to work primarily with borrowing/ lending and with giving/receiving. Buying/selling didn't seem to be where we could be the most useful at the time. We began to form our purposes as we studied. It soon became obvious that studying money had to go side by side with doing something practical that involved money. Every concept we explored cried out for a practical application. We needed a client who was doing something worthwhile and needed money. It was as simple as that. We yearned to demonstrate our ideals in practice.

Rudolf Steiner gave the Waldorf schools a spirit-filled curriculum. He enlivened the arts with his insights and spiritual teachings. He brought spirit into work with the land for farmers to practice not just sustainable agriculture but also a restorative agriculture, one that would renew the forces of the earth, even to bring spiritual nourishment into nutrition.

As we studied and searched for inspiration, we gradually discovered that we wanted to bring the living spirit into the movement of money. We realized that we could not do it alone, and that working in this way would become a life-long pursuit, possibly over many lifetimes.

We needed a vehicle to use for getting into those financial transactions through practical applications. The deeper we dove into questions and insights, the more we longed to take some practical actions. We also began to come to some tentative conclusions. These conclusions certainly gave us "a-ha" experiences, but they went deeper. They became some of the spiritual guidelines, governing our behaviors and the practices that eventually have become the hallmark of RSF. Simply put these conclusions are:

1. There is a difference between taking initiative and financing it. It is not the role of financiers to determine what happens in the world. Bankers search for initiative in others, select the ones they feel drawn to, and facilitate the flow of money to help realize these initiatives in life. Bankers are servants not leaders. Bankers lead through serving. Though RSF was not planning to be a bank, but a financial services organization, it also needed to consider the public benefit of its financial activities. If RSF was going to lend funds to worthy projects as part of its charitable mission, it needed to honor this insight of service in all its relations with clients.

2. Collateral in land and material assets is inferior to collateral in people and their strength of commitment. Securing the material collateral only preserves it from being taken over by another party. We wanted to protect our clients from any loss of their assets by unfriendly entities. Thus we did not want to rely only on the land and buildings for security for our loans. RSF had to find ways to harness people collateral for financing purposes. It needed to connect financial services with communities of people serving social ideals in practical ways.

3. Making money should not be our objective, but only the means to sustainability and rendering service. Our objectives must always be to serve initiative as it arises in human beings. We would charge fees only to support the RSF in its work, not to enrich any individual or group.

4. Helping clients become conscious of their interdependence creates a framework for building community and for knitting them all together into a fabric of common social perspective with diverse practical purposes. As such, we needed to build an educational component into our practical deeds. The right relationship and mutual understanding between all parties is critical for ensuring everyone's survival and growth. Every loan RSF makes should be based on a sound relationship of trust and mutual support. After all, RSF shouldn't be making a loan unless it wanted the borrowing project to succeed. That meant many financial transactions required advisory assistance as a means to become creditworthy.

5. In order to lend funds to a worthy project, RSF would have to acquire capital. It was conjectured that many people would be interested in having their savings support projects that were aligned with their values. Why not make it possible for people and organizations to open investment funds in RSF for the purpose of funding projects aligned with their values? RSF could be a values-driven investment organism funded by people and organizations cherishing similar values.

6. Although interest and fees increase the cost of a loan, it was the only way to make RSF sustainable. A fixed interest rate for a loan over a period meant ultimately that either RSF or the borrowing client would benefit at the expense of the other. We looked for a way for both to come out ahead, neither one at the expense of the other. At that time we charged only a variable interest rate. What made it socially constructive was that RSF would charge the same variable interest rate to the borrowing clients as would be paid to the investment fund clients. To cover RSF operating expenses we would charge both the investors and the borrowers a fee. Any organization that borrowed from RSF would become aware of the fact that RSF only had this money to lend because many supporting people and organizations chose to invest in projects such as theirs. Once, at the end of every year, we decided to supply the borrowers with a list of all the individuals and organizations that had made their loan possible. The amounts were not revealed, but only the names of those that made the loan possible. Excluded were only those who insisted on anonymity. The intention was to build community

around the sharing of resources used to accomplish worthwhile projects.

7. Finally, we agreed that, in keeping with the spirit of the time, we were not interested in working solely with those organizations devoted to the world impulse of Rudolf Steiner. We wanted to recognize worthwhile projects that were socially constructive and initiated by any individual or mission consistent organization. We felt it important to be as open as possible to what came to meet us out of the flow of this time. The study and focus on the wonderful work of Rudolf Steiner would be useful as a basis for engagement with the world, but not as dogma or creed that would limit RSF relationships or potential impact on the world.

John Alexandra began working on the internal accounting system, to make it transaction based and sensitive to the transactional nuances we wanted to incorporate in the client statements and reports. We wanted our clients to be able to see what their money was doing in the world when reading their statements. Ann Stahl began by assisting John and preparing and operating a small office in John's garage in Spring Valley, New York. Mark and I began focusing on sources of funding and potential clients. We used a small room in my home in Chatham, New York. Our job was to become the face of the enterprise, while John and Ann worked on the internal structures to sustain and make any work of RSF practical and secure.

45. WHY A FOUNDATION?

B EFORE WE WOULD be able to begin the work and actually make a loan, offer an investment account, advise an organization, and ask donors to help us get started, we needed a legal form and a name. The legal forms of a foundation at that time seemed narrow and inflexible. Essentially, they were set up to accumulate and preserve large amounts of capital that would earn income, which could be given away to worthwhile causes. It was obvious that the more capital in a foundation the higher the earnings. To make significant grants to worthwhile causes required a considerable amount of capital. Let's assume that $1 million dollars could earn on average 5%, or $50,000. If inflation ate away at the value of the capital, it meant that some of the earnings needed to be retained to offset the erosion caused by inflation. Then, assuming that inflation was less than 5%, only the difference between the earnings and the inflation rate could be used to make grants. This meant that a large amount of capital produced only a small amount of give-away income beyond what the IRS required.

The result was that the staff of any foundation is under great pressure to earn more than the rate of inflation. To earn more than the rate of inflation requires a relatively sophisticated investment team with high regard for growth and earnings. Many large foundations develop highly compensated investment teams and relatively modestly compensated program employees. Giving away the money is not as important to the organization as making it and growing the capital base. The financial structure of foundations rewards staff for keeping its resources and growing it. In the United States, only about 15% of the $2 trillion donated each year comes from foundations and businesses. Individuals donate about 85%. One can understand why.

So many foundations strive for earnings and growth, that fiduciary responsibility has come to mean investing safely for the highest returns. Very little concern at that time for the nature of such investments existed. Only recently has the issue of mission related investments come to the surface partly due to RSF and similar organizations. Why should a charitable organization give away a small percent of its earnings to support worthwhile projects, while the bulk, or roughly 95% of its capital, is invested in who knows what for the highest return? Under that structure, it is entirely possible for a foundation to award a grant of $500,000 to promote peace in the world, while $10 million could be invested in an arms manufacturer or other business earning good returns. While this example is somewhat exaggerated, it does illustrate the point.

The foundation legal form required a huge amount of capital working who-knows-where and for what purpose in the economy in order to provide a trickle of benefit to society. It didn't seem like quite the right form for achieving our goals. However, the Rudolf Steiner Foundation already existed. It was incorporated in the State of New York in 1934. Its main purpose was to receive the remainder of an estate, which included some property, on behalf of the Anthroposophical Society in America. The treasurer of the Anthroposophical Society was automatically a trustee of the Rudolf Steiner Foundation. Since I was the treasurer of the Society in 1981, I was therefore a trustee of the Rudolf Steiner Foundation.

The founding group decided to adopt the incorporated structure of the Foundation and transform it into an active social instrument. There remained $6,000 in the account of the RSF, which would soon be donated to a cancer research clinic in Switzerland. We knew this amount would soon be gone and we would have a zero balance in the RSF account.

46. THE CALL

IN LATE 1983, the Pine Hill Waldorf School in Wilton, New Hampshire, burned to the ground, leaving some 120 children and a dozen teachers without a home. The first tangible assignment of RSF was to work with this homeless school. The two founders and leading teachers of the school were karmically connected with me. One, Ann Courtney Pratt, was my classmate at High Mowing School, a boarding Waldorf school in the same town in New Hampshire. The other, Daniella Patrick Rettig, participated with me in a study group in New York City and was a dear friend. The call for help was a call out of karmic connections reaching into the distant past and could not be ignored. Moreover, the founders of RSF were eager to take on a project and welcomed this challenge with enthusiasm.

The RSF volunteers piled into a single car and traveled to New Hampshire. It was exciting to have a first opportunity to fumble with the words that conveyed the RSF mission and purpose. We met with the teachers, an architect that had returned from England to answer the call, and many of the parents. In the face of this tragedy, we were astounded by the forward-looking determination of those people. There was no doubt they wanted to rebuild and continue as a school. Every person who spoke to us was able to describe in vivid pictures what kind of facility they longed to build. Even the children had drawn pictures of their wishes for a school. The architect summarized the elements as connectivity to nature, filled with light and open space, humanly proportioned and not box-like. He then began putting the school community's dreams into architectural drawings.

RSF participated in an all school meeting in which many expressed their enthusiasm and determination to rebuild and flourish. High Mowing School, the sister school in the same town offered forty-five acres of its land across the road from its campus. High Mowing felt that land would not be needed by them and welcomed Pine Hill Waldorf School to become a close neighbor with common philosophical, ideological and educational approaches. All of these fortuitous happenings boded well for the future. One of the teachers, Arthur Auer, who was on sabbatical leave agreed to spearhead the project along with active trustees of the school. RSF volunteers acquired a growing confidence in the people and the project.

Life sometimes gives us very little chance to get ready for the challenges that face us. At the time the RSF volunteers plunged naively into these unknown responsibilities out of sheer love and enthusiasm. Challenges bring out of people what is necessary to deal with the challenges. No one would ever grow if not faced with the unasked-for challenges of life. The world of necessity, what we are challenged with, makes us creative and brings out the hidden talents and purposes that lie deep in our souls. *We become free in how we respond.* The world of necessity comes at us from without as though it is not part of us but the moment we are so confronted we have extraordinary freedom in how we respond. It is possible that whatever freedom we have is a gift from the necessities we are forced to deal with.

The RSF volunteers returned to New York and we pondered what we had done. We had promised to help with a loan of $500,000! We wondered how we were going to do that. The $6,000 had been sent to the cancer research clinic in Switzerland and there was no money in the RSF account.

The fact that all of us fell in love with Pine Hill Waldorf School turned out to be an important lesson and provided us with a significant operating procedure. From then on we always divided into two groups so that some of us visited the project and others stayed behind, in the office. It was realized that every time any of us advised or visited a project a wonderful process of seduction would be put into motion. We realized that leading with the heart had a natural consequence of falling in love with the wonderful people in the project and would lead to an intense desire to help.

It was decided that, whenever possible, no one from RSF would go alone to visit a project. There would always be a second person along to supplement and adjust the process as it evolved. Moreover, RSF would need a process back in the home office that was called "cold" to offset the impact of the "warm" site visit. It was reasoned that falling in love with the client was inevitable and RSF needed to institutionalize the counter balance in order to maintain objectivity and balance. These decisions contributed greatly to the ultimate success of RSF.

RSF began with a project in need, a life situation that required money to flow, to move. *This wonderful work did not begin with the acquisition of money but with the recognition of a need and by facilitating the movement of money in the service of life.* The project and its need seemed to pull in the investors and that began the special RSF way of working with money.

47. THE SUPPORT

RSF AS THE lender had to make visible the need for funds to support the rebuilding project of the Pine Hill Waldorf School. Thus RSF found it necessary to ask for support, not for itself, but for a worthwhile project. RSF was only the reliable intermediary to facilitate the movement of money from where it was less needed to where it was more needed. Relationships matter immensely and always will. Mary Theodora Richards, an elderly woman and a friend of my family whom we had chosen to care for in our home, heard all the conversations regarding the Pine Hill Waldorf School's situation. She had experienced the formation and creation of a mission for RSF. She now responded out of her immense desire to help and made the first "investment" in RSF.

It is interesting to note the karmic circumstances surrounding the meeting with Theodora Richards, as she liked to be called. At one time, I had the opportunity to operate a biodynamic food coop out of our apartment in New York City. People interested in such food placed their order every week. A truck would deliver the food in bulk. I remember filling the elevator several times while other tenants in the building waited patiently or eventually not so patiently. To our surprise, our coop grew dramatically. Within a matter of weeks we had to fill as many as seventy-eight orders. One day when the truck delivered, we had to make five or more trips in the elevator. Then my wife and I broke the bulk amounts into each order, did the billing, and by late afternoon people began arriving to pay and pick up their orders.

The superintendent of the building warned us that we couldn't go on doing our business out of a residential apartment. Down the street from us was a vacant little store measuring twenty feet by fifteen feet. We decided to rent it and operate the coop from the store once a week. The business grew and we were forced to open it on a second day and eventually had it open five days a week and began to make deliveries ourselves to people's apartments all over Manhattan, as well as other boroughs and even New Jersey along the Hudson River.

One day, a station wagon arrived at the store, delivering one dozen lettuce heads, each wrapped in tissue paper. They had obviously been harvested that morning and were as precious as gold. They had come from a farm in Chester, New York, run by two women, Marjorie Spock and Theodora Richards. Both were very active in the biodynamic/organic movement and had done a great deal of research on the harmful effects of pesticides and artificial fertilizers. They were among the first biodynamic farmers in America and provided their research to Rachel Carson for her book *The Silent Spring.*

Our store became so popular that we met with several suppliers and considered the idea of opening a biodynamic supermarket. Two of the suppliers offered to form a partnership with me. We each would capitalize the market with $5,000, which would give us a total of $15,000 to start. That would cover the rent, utilities, and other expenses for six months. I traveled to the farm of Marjorie Spock and Theodora Richards and described the project to them. Theodora was excited about opening the first biodynamic supermarket in New York City, and when I left I had a check in my pocket for $5,000, a personal gift to me to cover my share of the partnership.

During the following weeks, the partners met several times. Each time new wrinkles developed in our relationship. At one time it began to look like my $5,000 was going to be the only cash invested; the other partners would put up services and goods of one kind or another. I became uneasy and consulted a friend who was very blunt; he advised, "If there is the slightest mistrust, don't do it!" I eventually decided not to go ahead with the idea. It was still a good idea, but the risks seemed too one-sided, and I was not a hundred percent sure that my career path was to be a grocer. I informed the other two that I was backing out. There was great disappointment all around and we parted ways. Karma apparently has an infinite number of sides and nuances to it.

I returned the check for $5,000 to Theodora Richards and earned the dubious honor of being the first person ever to return a gift to her. We became good friends, and when she needed a place and people to care for her many years later, we offered our home in Chatham, New York, to her. That is the story of how Theodora Richards came to live in our home and take an interest in the creation of RSF. The founders of RSF had conceived the idea of transforming the Foundation into a vehicle for Investors and Borrowers to become conscious of one another and together make money move in socially constructive ways. We imagined many people desiring social change investing in RSF and being informed of worthwhile projects, which their funds were making possible. Theodora Richards became the first investor in RSF. She was thrilled with the idea that she could be helping RSF do its work while simultaneously helping the Pine Hill Waldorf School. She also marveled at the idea that lending could become charitable as well as giving.

We found that by speaking everywhere on behalf of the Pine Hill Waldorf School other people began to lend RSF their savings to use in funding such a worthwhile project. Without any money of its own and without any credit, using the money invested in RSF by socially conscious human beings in turn enabled the RSF to finance a loan of $500,000 to the Pine Hill Waldorf School. Recently at a ceremony that celebrated the successful history and current accomplishments of the Pine Hill Waldorf School special thanks were given to RSF, which bridged the crisis faced by the school and helped them to move into their beautiful facilities. At the same time I was also able to thank the Pine Hill Waldorf School and give it credit for launching RSF toward its remarkable growth and service. How fruitful work can be when karma among the people is healthy and leads to collaborative work. I began to base most of my judgments, business, as well as personal on a sensing of the karmic connections revealed in action.

Today, some twenty plus years later, more than 800 individuals and organizations have invested about $60 million in RSF in carefully managed Investment Funds so that worthwhile projects could be financed successfully. During those more than twenty years, almost $100 million has been loaned out doing good work in society. The results are visible all over the United States and in other countries as well. The loans are of course repaid over time, so the $100 million has turned over several times. That's the wonderful side effect of such an investment. It is like getting triple or quadruple social mileage out of the same funds. From its position as intermediary, RSF can observe the movement of money enveloped by the ideals and values of the investors, as it brings about socially constructive projects. Deficits have been overcome and financial health restored, auditoriums, gymnasiums, arts buildings, classrooms, and many other projects have been accomplished, many times by non-profit organizations the banks were afraid to finance.

And how do the non-profit 501(c)(3) clients pay back the loans to RSF? Schools rarely show a profit in their operations. The activity of providing new human capacities for society through the education of children seems never to have enough funds. The way schools repay their loans is usually through soliciting gifts from parents, alumni, and friends to supplement what they can repay out of operations. So, in addition to providing the funds for growth in education, $100 million in loans turned over three times, the same funds have stimulated probably about another $300 million in gifts to pay principal and fees. If the lending process is correctly structured it stimulates the collective charitable impulses of people and organizations all over the world.

The $500,000 RSF loaned to the Pine Hill Waldorf School was accompanied by a great deal of advice and working together on a capital campaign to supplement and repay the loan. All the parents willingly signed a legally binding pledge for any amount they could afford. Some made outright gifts and others pledged an amount to be paid every month for three years. Still others made quarterly payments. The school also printed 200 non-negotiable, interest-free bonds that could be redeemed if another parent purchased them or they could eventually be given to the school for a tax deduction.

What was this innovative structure that RSF created to take the money out of pure finance and place it into social healing? We called this approach a pledge community. RSF invented the idea of pledge communities to collateralize a loan as well as repaying it. The concept is that the safety of any loan is secured through the power of determined cooperation in a community around a project. If every member absorbs some risk and commits to a specified contribution over time, the loan is repaid with everyone sharing in its repayment according to each person's ability. If, for example, 200 families and friends around a school or other non-profit organization all pledge monthly, quarterly or yearly contributions over a three-year period, in many cases the total of such pledged amounts is sizeable. RSF uses those pledges both as collateral or sometimes partial collateral for the loan, as well as repayment of the debt.

This is community building, not as a focus group training exercise, but in real time. Each person who pledges relies on every other one; they all depend on each other to satisfy the requirements of the loan and realize their common dream. They each become aware that they are the ones who build and maintain the facilities in which precious work is unfolding. It becomes "their" school. Thus every parent has a direct stake in the educational culture sustaining the school community.

In the twenty plus years since 1984 RSF has only experienced three defaults. Because of the community building structure supporting each of the loans, most of the funds were recovered. Donors who pledged honored their commitments. Up until the time of this writing, the total funds not repaid were much less than five tenths of one percent. This amount was charged to a guarantee fund, which RSF had the foresight to establish in its early years.

RSF wanted to provide a safety net for investors as well as donors. Since lending money to an organization, no matter how honorable or sustainable the organization is, involves risk, we needed to absorb the potential downside of such risks. Thus we created a fund—a guarantee fund that would protect RSF and its investment clients—and invited donors to participate. At any given time, the guarantee fund is of a size that could cushion RSF in the event of a potential, estimated loss.

In time RSF broadened its connection to social enterprise lending, including fair-trade-inspired organizations, indigenous design, and independent media, to name just a few. Eventually additional internal restructuring was necessary and subsidiary foundations were established to accommodate the increasing complexity of RSF's transactions and relationships. Thus was launched the social lending processes of RSF and the establishment of investment funds for those people and organizations interested in knowing what good their funds were doing in the world as well as earning a living return.

RSF maintains that money invested in RSF Investment Funds has a different quality to it. It has an aura of attentiveness and social concern around it. It moves in a health-giving tempo and seems to encounter those people and organizations that care about the future of human beings and their world. Money loaned to socially constructive projects is serious money. It is almost as if the money knows how important it is. The people, who sign various kinds of commitment documents such as promissory notes, pledge agreements or guarantees know that their signature is important and that the future health of the world relies on their commitment.

One time RSF made a precarious loan to a school with internal social problems. In a sense the risk was great but the chance that the school could overcome its difficulties and serve its parents and children seemed worth taking. Sixteen guarantors backed the loan. Within a year the school community broke apart and the school had to close. The parents all had to find other schools for the children; some even moved away, closer to a good school. The sixteen guarantors all paid their guarantees, even though their children were in other schools and the emotional trauma around the closing was acute. In the course of all the loan discussions, the risks had been carefully explored and acknowledged and it was understood that the loan was only possible because many other people had invested in RSF and might suffer in the event of default. The guarantors all paid up their guarantee amount.

48. Assisting Donors

WHILE THE INVOLVEMENT of RSF in the transactions of lending/borrowing was driven by worthwhile projects, the giving/receiving area of RSF's work came about through relationships with Donors. RSF discovered the form of a "donor advised fund." It enables a donor to give funds to RSF into a segregated fund, which earns interest and remains subject to recommendations for its disposition from the initial donor or a designated advisor. RSF acknowledges receipt of the recommendation, performs due diligence, and if appropriate, makes the grant to the designated recipient.

Theodora Richards opened the first investment fund at RSF. She also opened the first donor advised fund. This saved her the work of correspondence and check writing to other organizations. Her part of the work was completed once she had made the recommendation to RSF. She previously made a number of small gifts at specific times of the year to a number of charitable projects and organizations. RSF was of significant service to her in that she simply recommended grants to be made out of her donor advised fund and RSF performed all the due diligence and made the actual grant transactions.

Although Theodora Richards was the first, she was not the only one. RSF found that donors were in need of assistance in wonderful and surprising ways. Many donors found the donor advised fund form useful. For some it was expedient to make a gift at a certain time of year for tax reasons. Because they did not yet know where their gifts were the most needed, they gave their money to RSF in a donor advised fund and later recommended recipients of their funds. By the time of this writing more than $30 million of RSF assets are in donor advised funds. It is a growing segment of RSF activity as donors discover the advantages and convenience of this useful form.

The grant-making activity of RSF received a boost largely due to the number of donor advised funds. More recently there has been a proliferation of various charitable funds, some of which were created in response to direct gifts of donors to support certain grants and charitable endeavors. RSF has been able to support workshops, seminars, meetings, and conferences on money, and spirit and money. The expansion of its rented offices with the larger conference room in the Presidio in San Francisco made it possible for RSF to hold meetings of mission related organizations on its premises.

49. INTERCONNECTIONS

THE RELATIONSHIPS BETWEEN investors and RSF, between donors and RSF, and between borrowers and RSF multiplied and generated a great deal of activity. RSF pictured itself as the facilitator of community building around loans and donors. It wasn't until later that a new dimension of this community-building exercise became evident. The possibility of investors and donors working together around a project, or borrowers and recipients finding common ground for mutual work was not in the original concept. However, reality often produces unexpected hybrids. Once a few examples materialized, it was easier to understand what this new inter-connectivity meant.

A small Waldorf school had a surplus of $1,000 at the end of its fiscal year. The board debated what to do with it. Finally they decided they would open an investment fund in RSF with it, because while they did not need it right away, they hoped it would be used to fund other worthy projects. This was the first case of schools helping schools. The example suggested that schools could work together, lend each other funds through RSF for worthy projects and still receive a modest but secure return. The idea of mission-related investing was born out of practice. It was a question of trusting a sister organization to take the risk. RSF as intermediary could be the third party in such relationships, ensuring proper documentation, arm's-length objectivity, and an element of risk management. Eventually other organizations began to see the potential in working together with RSF and each other. Organic and biodynamic farms have this potential, as do holistic medical practices, foundations, and businesses.

Another school put their small endowment into an investment fund at RSF. Their fund made a number of socially constructive projects possible. The interest paid by the projects enabled the school's endowment fund to give tuition assistance and scholarships to worthy students in the school. Slowly the idea began to flourish among our clients that we are all interconnected through the movement of our money and that if we are conscious of how our money enables constructive work, it moves with an aura of hope and enlightenment attached to it. The movement of money is "charged" with the value-based intentions of socially conscious individuals and organizations. Remember that every financial transaction requires agreement between two parties. It is in the agreement-forming process that social values are acknowledged which eventually lead to the creation of an economic value.

A teacher received an inheritance and wanted to make a somewhat larger gift toward her school's capital campaign. However, she was concerned that such a gift might distort or negatively affect her relationship with her colleagues. She opened a donor advised fund in RSF, where it continued to earn by partially helping to fund a project. While it was still intact, she was pleased that it was doing something connected with her own values. Eventually she then recommended a gift be made to her school anonymously. In this way her inheritance served multiple goals and still preserved her anonymity and relationships with colleagues.

A foundation that made annual gifts to many worthy projects each year opened an investment fund in RSF and was pleased that this part of their large investment portfolio was mission related. At least this part of their portfolio could be identified as furthering their charitable purposes. That investment enabled RSF to make loans to worthy projects, which in turn paid interest and fees that enabled the source foundation to make its gifts and support RSF and its work.

The whole chain of interconnectivity has been remarkable. Individuals and organizations funded investment funds in RSF and RSF made loans to worthy projects. The worthy projects paid interest that enabled the Investors to continue their good work. The projects also paid fees that supported RSF in its work. It made so much sense to know what our money was doing in the world, where it was working, and who was supported and helped. The movement of money began to be a healing force, a healing circulation that countered some of the other coagulating symptoms in the world economy. Money that coagulates out of the flow, out of the movement around the globe becomes available to lend and give, but most of us hold on to it with a fear that we might not have enough. That's a legitimate concern for some of our resources. However, there is really no way to hold on to it. It's a question of who do we trust to use it, the bank, a business, a mutual fund? In all those cases we don't really know what they are stimulating in the world economy. For people who want to know what their money is doing, RSF and now other similar organizations is an alternative party for their socially constructive investment agreements.

This new revelation about the interconnectivity of all our clients and their values also made us understand the connections between ultimate goals and the means for achieving them. Once a noble intention finds its vivid clarity and once a number of socially awake individuals connect with it; there are many possibilities for moving money constructively. Investing provides funds for achieving social goals. Lending permits certain steps to occur which can launch a worthy endeavor. Giving can be done in a healthy way directly associated with a planned project without any social short circuits. In other words, lending, investing, borrowing, giving and receiving can all be charitable in their nature and can accomplish innovative social projects. For RSF the new motto of innovative social finance was born.

50. WHY WALDORF SCHOOLS?

ORIGINALLY, RSF FOCUSED much of its lending activity on Waldorf and Waldorf-inspired schools, although there were also projects with biodynamic/organic farms, holistic medical practices and similar projects. RSF has been involved with more than one hundred Waldorf and Waldorf-inspired schools in North America. All together, since 1984 RSF has loaned about $55 million to Waldorf and Waldorf-inspired school projects. During the same time, approximately $60 million in gifts to schools and compatible organizations in North America were facilitated.

In 1984, there were only about ninety-five Waldorf schools in North America. Today there are nearly two hundred, a growth of more than a hundred percent. This means an average of some five new schools every year. At that time in 1984, there were about 7,000 students attending the schools and approximately 460 teachers and staff. Today we understand that there are approximately 30,000 students enrolled and some 1,350 teachers and staff engaged in the wonderful work of educating children for the future.

Some aspects of the growth in Waldorf schools that readers may not be familiar with are vital to the work of RSF. Twenty plus years ago, the total assets of the Waldorf school movement in North America was estimated to be about $50 million. Today the assets are nearly $900 million. Inflation accounts for some of this growth in asset value, but the bulk of it is due to the increased level of acquisition of property and construction that has accompanied the growth of the schools these last twenty plus years.

Much of the $55 million loaned to the Waldorf schools has been paid back and new loans made. Very rarely has a school been able to carry large debt service over long periods. Every loan made has the side effect of increasing the donations and gifts made to the school to liquidate the loan as quickly as possible. Some 45,600 parents not only carry the annual budgets of the independent Waldorf schools, which amount to about $200,000,000, but they also carry the immense gift stream that helps to reduce the indebtedness of the schools and makes possible a steady list of improvements and capital projects on existing facilities.

The Waldorf school movement is sizeable and influential. The parents and friends of the schools are a major factor in the green economy. They tend to purchase organic/ biodynamic foods, value natural products and alternative, integrative doctors and medicines and are culturally classical. Beyond these statistics, it is obvious that how the Waldorf schools educate children is not only unique, it is evolutionary. In a time when most of our educational practices come out of antiquated concepts and methods, it might very well be the only curriculum and approach to education that meets the demands of our modern age. It seems natural that RSF, an organization that offers innovative social finance should harmonize with Waldorf schools that offer an innovative social education.

51. RENEWED LEADERSHIP

IN 1992, MARK Finser was elected to the presidency of RSF. This represented a renewal of the existing leadership approach. Mark brought a more modern, cosmopolitan view to RSF ideals, in that he wished the foundation to be in the public eye and influencing how people view their money and work with its affects on our social life. He wanted growth in assets and social impact, but also wanted RSF to intermingle with like-minded individuals and organizations. He wanted RSF to recognize its intimate connection with others who carry similar ideals and intentions to bring about change in how the world works with money.

It is almost impossible to describe adequately the difference Mark's leadership meant for RSF. His breadth of vision, warmth of soul and determined connectivity with every human being he encountered gave RSF a remarkable texture and feel to it. He drew people into connection with RSF and did it by taking their interests to heart. He is one of those very few individuals who are able to serve everyone else's intentions while not abandoning his own integrity and purpose. Each of his contacts felt trusted and supported by Mark and in response he was trusted and supported and RSF grew and grew.

The next four years marked considerable growth to the point where RSF no longer fit into the rent-free space provided by the Anthroposophical Society. In 1994, RSF purchased its own building in Harlemville, New York, and continued to grow in every conceivable measure. In 1997, at the November trustee meeting, RSF considered a proposal by Mark to move the home office to San Francisco. With endless questions and cautions, the decision was made, and in April 1998 RSF landed at its present address in the Presidio, San Francisco. The presidio was once a military base balanced on the hills overlooking the Golden Gate Bridge and the shipping lanes into San Francisco harbor. In the mid-1990s, it became a national park managed by a trust that determines its uses. From a few offices, the continued growth of RSF required in 2005 that it absorb the entire building at 1002A and B at the Presidio. A new life began for RSF in the exciting city of San Francisco.

52. Articulating the Mission

THE MEANING OF our time becomes clear when we learn to take heart and look deeper at the currents in our culture. The numbers in RSF statements tell us that we are making a difference. We are transforming the world, if ever so slowly but surely. We are finding friends in each other and in larger circles whose values are coinciding with ours. The numbers say to us that the world is changing and that a future filled with warmth and light is slowly being germinated amidst the chaos of our time. RSF is participating in the rising of a new phoenix from the media distorted reality of our time.

In its various publications and materials, and on the website rsfsocialfinance.org the mission and activities are described in detail. Some statements I have found interesting are quoted below:

> RSF creates social benefit through innovative approaches to working with money that reflect the highest aspirations of the human spirit. We foster relationships, collaboration, and community building as the basis for the movement of money and the cultivation of living economies.

> RSF provides ways for donors, investors, borrowers, and grant recipients to use money to integrate their values with practical objectives. To further this mission, RSF carries out its services on a worldwide basis through philanthropic management, community investment, lending, grant-making, advising and educational programs.

Funding areas include:

> Children and education
> Environment and sciences
> Sustainable agriculture
> Arts and culture
> Economic and social renewal
> Disadvantaged communities

> Medicine and healing
> Spiritual and religious renewal

Again, the source of much of its inspiration and dedication is acknowledged with the words, "RSF is inspired by the insights of Rudolf Steiner, an innovative and far-reaching social philosopher of the early twentieth century. He encouraged human beings to practice self-knowledge in order to rise above materialism and to take responsibility for the condition of the world. RSF accepts this responsibility by working with the social principles of freedom in cultural life, equality in political affairs, and interdependence in a sustainable economy."

In the last seven years, RSF has discovered how many friends it has in the world, and how many individuals and organizations are compatible with its mission. RSF has expanded its educational efforts and formed alliances with compatible endeavors and now enjoys working together with so many other human beings striving to change how the world works with money. It would be impossible to name them all, as the list is incredibly long.

In 2006, with a staff of twenty-four highly competent and dedicated individuals drawn from all walks of life, RSF is expanding into alliances with many organizations and discovering how widespread is the search and yearning for spirit in the practical life of our time. The employees and trustees discover through conversations in airplanes, trains and in meetings with bankers, business people and successful performers and politicians that spirit and money matter and the two are a powerful blend for transforming our social life. To learn more about RSF, its mission and alliances, visit the interactive web site at rsfsocialfinance.org.

THE FUTURE

53. The Past

Looking at the human evolutionary process from ancient times through Greece, Rome, and the Renaissance, we see how we were gradually weaned from our dependency on spiritual powers that slowly relinquished their authority over our conduct. In the Norse myths we are portrayed as children of the gods; in ancient Greece the gods and humans are on the same stage; in ancient Rome the gods are found only in the temples and oracles; finally in the Renaissance, the gods are no longer present in our daily lives and seem to have abandoned us, except to inspire us through creative ideas.

This sequence describes a clear path of development: the gods fading from prominence, and human beings developing toward center stage where we are today. The description of this path has been handed down orally through stories until we reached the point where we begin to have records and written accounts. The myth of Loki, the *Iliad*, and the "Last King of Rome" are examples of this path. During that long course of events we developed, but not all together because almost all the stages of development are still to be experienced in various peoples on the earth at this time.

When we read or hear accounts of wanton genocide in an African territory, consider that the different stages of consciousness are in evidence in that area. There are clearly those who feel the gods are acting with them in support of their violent actions. There are also those who try to lead toward less violent, negotiated solutions, and there are those who are disconnected and suffering at the hands of others who have weapons and appear to be at an earlier stage of consciousness. Wherever violence or genocide erupts, it is usually perpetrated by undereducated people enmeshed in power struggles between a few individuals who are still anchored in an ancient mentality of egoism. Eventually, in such territories and everywhere in the world, even they will change. Such behaviors and such self-aggrandizement are fading as human beings develop their sense of the worldwide human community. A sustainable future for humanity requires that we all need each other's differences and thrive in rights common to us all. Nothing ever happens in life without some leading the way while others hold back to lead at another time. In such a vast theatre as our earthly globe it is to be expected that as some move forward others hold on to an earlier consciousness and then move forward overtaking those more precocious elements and themselves leading for a time. In the development of humanity as in the development of individuals there is no prescribed lockstep.

Imagine how our country grew and was settled by energetic outcasts from European society. Even the most ruthless settlers in this country, those, who became the leading families, gradually acquired this new sense of community. Today, these same leading families are major benefactors of the cultural life. Those who made the national parks, the symphony orchestras, the major colleges, and universities were originally renegades and self-absorbed determined individualists. Perhaps the stage of egoism is necessary in order to develop into the altruism of the future.

Just as civilizations moved from East to West, from ancient India to Persia, to Egypt, then Greece, Rome, Central Europe and then to America, so do humans grow from a childlike state, to teenage self-absorption to rampant egoism and eventually to civic mindedness and community building. This is what I refer to as the stages of development in humankind. Of course, this is a very long-term view and requires us to include reincarnation as a given. After all, each of us has to be present at each major step in order that the effect is cumulative. I don't think it is possible for us to catch up on more than 10,000 years of human development in the few years of our childhood!

If our educational approach to children were designed to refresh our unconscious recall of past historical epochs, we might be more prepared for what we presently face as adults. The Waldorf school makes it a point to recapitulate for every child the historical development of humanity from myths to oral storytelling to biography to factual records and materials. Most graduates of such schools have the incredible experience of finally arriving in the present time, ready to jump in with all their faculties intact.

Even though we were incarnated in all the epochs of our evolution, it is still necessary to refresh our experiences as we grow into our present bodies. The fact that we repeatedly reincarnate simplifies education. We don't actually have to start from scratch each time we incarnate. We simply are the same people who were present in ancient Atlantis, ancient India, ancient Persia, Babylonia, Mesopotamia, and Egypt. Homer is describing us in the *Iliad* and the *Odyssey*. We were there in ancient Rome and during the Renaissance. History is so fascinating to many of us because we read and study our own earlier biographies. It shouldn't be called history, as though it describes the lives and deeds of somebody else. We should call it *OurStory*. Then we would have the right perspective on what we are doing as we investigate the past. Throughout the vast evolution of human culture on this planet, the land has been there, the plants, the animals, the air; all was here as a foundation for our growth. We have been provided a relatively stable stage on which to develop ourselves. If we can believe the myths and stories, we have even had a great deal of help along the way. That help was gradually withdrawn, not to punish us, but to allow us to develop.

It would be helpful if more of us made the effort to penetrate through our daily consciousness to a longer-term remembrance. It helps us to understand who we are in the context of who we were. Imagine how much richer and deeper our relationships would be if we included our memories from past lives and what we achieved or didn't achieve in earlier times. *OurStory* would be such a personal as well as an objective discovery process! Together and singly we developed, maturing in our capacities, able more and more to become conscious beings serving the long-term evolution of this remarkable being we call human. The future holds great promise if we can only develop to our full potential all that we are inherently capable of becoming.

For example can we imagine a time when any of us would be so aware of what is going on in the world that we couldn't bear to see another suffer without becoming involved in a helping way? Can we look forward a bit in our electronic age and realize that we can in an instant discharge funds to prevent another from misery or starvation. An excellent book to read is Lynn Twist's *The Soul of Money!* In her eloquent and persuasive book we experience an energetic proponent of sufficiency. It is an example of the possibility that we have the technical capability to form a healthy global community. Rudolf Steiner's social motto expresses this beautifully: "The healthy social life is found when in the mirror of each one of us the whole community finds its reflection and when in the community the virtue of each one is living."[1]

Such a healthy social life is within our reach. Are we ready to realize that potential? Do we have the all-encompassing vision of what it means to be human? Are we ready to take into our hands our own further development, now that the divine powers have brought us this far and have left the remainder of the course to our own forces of will and determination? The movement of money is tied to our own development. We grow and money will accompany our renewed sense of purpose. In what ways do we need to change and how will the movement of money be effected?

54. How Do We Change?

IF THE MOVEMENT of money will change when we change, then how do we change? Do we change because the environment requires it? Do we change when our genes have been altered either through heredity or through manipulation? The kind of change I am advocating is not inherent in the genes. Our environment may force us to change, but do we want to wait until we have no choice? Do we want the earth to become a kind of landfill, or do we want to pollute outer space with our debris? Isn't it time we produce the conditions we want on earth for our children and for ourselves in future incarnations? The changes I would like to see are possible to nurture in our souls. Our souls, capable of thinking, feeling, and willing can transform these capacities into rarer forms, forms we alone can create in ourselves in complete freedom.

Once, in New York City, I was accosted by a young couple who asked me for a dollar to buy some food, just to last through the night. I walked by, thinking they were young enough to work, healthy and able-bodied; why should I help them? I heard the girl say quietly to the man as they turned away despondently; "Don't give up. We'll make it."

I had already walked a dozen yards away, when I paused and thought, "Suppose I am wrong and they really do need some help? Is it my responsibility? They must have friends or relatives!" I tried to wiggle out of it. In the end, however, I realized that they had asked me. No matter what I chose to do, it would be my response to their request that entered my consciousness out of the world.

I reached into my pocket to see what money I had. In my hand was a twenty-dollar bill and some change. I wondered what good the change would do them and concluded probably no good at all. I found myself thinking, "Siegfried, either help them right now or leave them in other hands." Then I turned back and the couple looked at me. They were a little apprehensive.

"What will you do?" I asked.

The girl said, "I don't know but after we eat something we will fig-ure it out." She did look hungry, so I gave her the twenty-dollar bill.

She said, "Thank you," and then saw that it was twenty dollars and not just a dollar bill. "Look!" she said to her man, "look what it is!" Then she turned to really thank me, but I was already down the street.

This was one of the few times I really felt good about giving money to someone. Mostly I feel put upon, begrudging what I give, because I don't believe the story I am told. This time, I felt connected with the stream of humanity and knew, really knew I had done the right thing.

What happened to the young couple? I wanted confirmation so in about ten minutes I walked back to where they had been. There was no sign of them. I looked across the street to a coffee shop that was still open. Crossing the street I glanced over my shoulder into the coffee shop. They were there close together looking at the money, discussing various options and prices, I suppose. Glad to be confirmed in my choice, I resumed my walk. Was I twenty dollars poorer or was I immeasurably richer? That's the thing about a gift; you never know its value until often many years later. In this case, I never met the same couple again, at least not to my knowledge. Who knows, they may have turned out to be one of my clients thirty or forty years later?

This little story is only one personal experience that showed me we can be more meaningful in our actions by deepening our feeling and being more deliberate about what we do. I could have tossed a few coins at them, almost annoyed that they accosted me. In another case, that might have been the right thing to do, but I felt something in our encounter I was reluctant to ignore; something in our relationship was crying out for attention. Such feelings matter because they may be echoing from another lifetime or an earlier part of this life that eludes our consciousness.

How can we live a life that acknowledges our nuances of feeling, often carrying messages of a past life and how can we act in such a way that we invest in each moment the healing forces we are capable of generating? Goethe provided us with an insight on this question in a revealing fairy tale he wrote near the end of his life. One of the characters in his fairy tale, *The Green Snake and the Beautiful Lily*, expressed these wise words.

"What is more precious than gold?"
"The light!" comes the answer.
"What is more precious than light?"
"Conversation" is the answer.[2]

Goethe knew that dialogue and discourse bring us out of isolation and into community together. Our consciousness is raised while we build relationships that endure around the achieving of our deepest intentions.

In these words Goethe expresses that light can come in isolation. That is why we say, "I see" when we suddenly understand something. We mean that our soul has thrown light on something we couldn't see before, something that was in the dark. He also expresses that we can progress only so far by ourselves and then run into dead ends or lose ourselves in abstractions. Goethe tells us that the sheer presence of another human thinking, feeling and willing with us creates true social motion into the unknown. Knowledge changes and becomes wisdom when we are in real conversation.

Commitment to personal transformation is essential. How do we change? How do we grow and become? There is a simple answer: "Not alone!" When we study or consider our goals by ourselves, we evolve ideas and thoughts that have a natural tendency to disconnect from the reality. True, only when we are alone can we form the world according to our liking and become finally clear. However, what good is that if it works differently in the actual world or if we will have to force our clear conclusions on the reality? Only in conversation with others, not chitchat, but about what matters to us, do we wake up to the other and to ourselves. Meaningful conversation is not transmittal of information like E-mail, or even "snail mail." Meaningful conversation is one world engaging with another world in a common social sphere perceivable to both. I struggle to communicate with you. You struggle to understand what I am trying to describe. Because you are listening to me I discover more in what I was trying to express than I knew was there. You suddenly catch a glimpse of what is living in our conversation and something awakens in you that was not fully conscious before. It is catching and I wake up to the current between us and change. Change or growth or development is what can result from a conversational/listening engagement with another human being.

John Alexandra and I had such conversations all through 1983 in Hamburger Heaven. At that time we wondered what could be done to bring spirit into the movement of money. Our meetings were always early in the morning before Wall Street woke up. Over breakfast we pondered not only the state of the world, but our own capacities and ideals. How much were we willing and able to sacrifice. All meaningful endeavors in a real world require sacrifice and those willing to sacrifice qualify themselves as initiators in the name of the spirit. To further such an initiative as RSF we needed to be open and invite the gods or spirit, back into our world. It is not easy to invite someone you are not sure really exists. It requires some inner wrestling to resolve that question.

I am not sure that blind belief in an angel or other spiritual being will really do it anymore for most of us. We have reached the stage where knowing is more convincing than believing. I had to find my way, earlier in life, to an understanding of how spirit relates to matter. To me, the world presents itself from two directions. First, the world presents itself through our senses. The various instruments that facilitate the sense perceptions are just extensions of our senses. A telescope is only an extension of my eyes. Chemical analysis is simply an extension of our sense of touch and smell and taste. All our inventions or at least most of them are an extension of our ears, our eyes, and the other senses. That is one way the world presents the information we need for the conduct of life.

However, what our senses bring us is disorganized. It is chaotic and rich but incomprehensible without the second source of information. Our capacities to think, feel, and will are absolutely necessary to organize our sense impressions into a comprehensible wholeness in which we can dare to move and exist. At least that is the case presently with the consciousness we currently have as adults. Children grow into this consciousness and gradually become skilled in doing, feeling, and thinking in order to become adult. These capacities to think, feel and will are not given to us in the same way as our body and sense organs are given. They only gradually develop over a period of some twenty-one years in an average human life. Other adults help us to develop these capacities. They develop in us within a social context as we mature. They develop in relationship to other humans with whom we are allowed to shape our lives and deal with what comes toward us.

These three capacities are soul powers, not body powers. They form themselves out of soul connections with other humans and flower in our social life together. To me these three are the purest evidence of spirit working in the human soul. You can't see feeling, or thinking or willing. They are all three invisible. In psychology the soul was thought of as the black box, meaning "the unknowable." It was generally understood that we cannot know what happens in the soul because it cannot be weighed, counted, or measured, or in the words of Edward L. Thorndike's proposition 6: "Whatever exists at all exists in some amount,"[3] therefore the soul cannot be known. He, in turn, was interpreting René Descartes and his *Principles of Philosophy*, "If something exists, it exists in some amount. If it exists in some amount, then it is capable of being measured."[4] As a result, psychologists and educators turned to something that could be weighed, counted, or measured, namely behavior. Hence came the idea of standardized tests and psychological research based on quantifiable data. I refer to the soul as the light-filled consciousness of our time that expresses itself in three ways, by thinking, feeling and willing. What enters in us and thrives or suffers in our soul is the spirit.

I have learned a great deal from the work of Rudolf Steiner who suggested many ways to cultivate still other capacities for dealing effectively with the world through what he called spiritual science. He gave some 6,000 lectures and wrote several hundred books, articles and published letters. His most productive years were the last thirteen. Rudolf Steiner died at age sixty-five, following a lifetime of devotion to the spirit of our time. I would recommend a recent book by Henry Barnes, *A Life for the Spirit,* to learn more about him and his work.

55. SPIRIT AND SOUL

I RESOLVED THE QUESTION of the existence of spirit for myself when I studied my biography, not so much from the point of view of what I accomplished, thought, and initiated, but more from the point of view of turning points in my life. I carefully reviewed every detail of each such turning point and came away with a whole new perspective. It seems at every turning point in my life my consciousness was just slightly lowered as a host of coincidences and accidents occurred with apparently highly choreographed effect, and I was not fully awake to what was happening. In retrospect, as I look back on such happenings, my memories reveal details I hadn't noticed before.

One example stands out in my memory. Once I was looking for a job after leaving my earlier employment as a teacher. At one point I was a bit discouraged because all the usual methods seemed not to work for me. I stood on a street corner trying to decide whether I should quit and go home, sit down in a coffee shop for energy renewal, or something more productive, I did not know what. Beside me was one of those large, metal wastebaskets one finds in New York City. I merely glanced down at it, but something caught my eye. It was the back page of a newspaper. "WANTED!" shouted to me in large print. I picked it out of the basket and read "Young men, personable and aggressive, desired for exciting career in advising businesses." The ad went on to describe the opportunity in more detail.

I had never known of such a career, having been a teacher for the last six years dealing daily with children and other teachers. It was exciting to think of advising businesses. How does one do that? I ripped out the ad and later that morning was interviewed. I was told I had to take a test. Fine, I had no problem with that! I was ushered into another room and sat down before a pencil and a small booklet of test questions. As was my usual approach, I glance at a few questions before starting. The questions all seemed to focus on how aggressive I was. If that's what they want, I can be aggressive, I thought. With every question I picked the most aggressive answer offered.

I was offered the job before I left. However, I became suspicious. Why does someone have to be that aggressive, and only aggressive? What ever happened to being perceptive and sensitive and other such qualities? I went to the public library and looked up the profession of advising and consulting. I found an Association of Consulting Engineers located near Grand Central Station. When I called the number, a cautious man would not tell me anything about the company that had just hired me, but he was willing to discuss it in person. When we met, he was very candid and made no bones about his opinion of my potential employer. He made it clear it was not the organization I wanted to join.

"The idea of advising businesses really interests me. I have never heard of that before. I'm disappointed that I won't have this chance" I mourned.

"Well," he said, "Maybe you should apply at a couple of really reputable consulting firms. I happen to know that Barrington and Company, right across the street, is looking for someone. They have just landed a consulting assignment with the Rochester School District and need someone with an educational background. Why not go there and apply?"

I did, and there met the man who would be my mentor for the next five years, teaching me everything he knew and at the same time also revealing to me who and what he was which was the real learning for me. I tell this story to show how I went from a newspaper ad in the garbage to a bad consulting firm to an association and then to a most exciting career advising clients, all through a series of accidents. The man in the Association of Consulting Engineers who advised me left his job before I could adequately thank him. He was there just for me, a complete stranger! Another afternoon and the garbage basket would have been emptied I am sure. All the connections were coincidental and illuminating for me. I look back at such events and I am filled with wonder and gratitude for the choreography that carried me along into my next phase of life. My life is filled with such choreography. True, I had to be a willing participant, which I was most of the time, and yet there is something moving in the patterns of my life that has wisdom in it. I feel I am in a motion filled pattern field that appears to be custom fitted for my benefit.

When I explored my feelings at each of those turning points, I found even more surprising influences. It turned out that I had complete confidence in what the moment would bring. I thought at first it was just that I was a very confident sort of guy. As I paused and explored more deeply such moments, I actually began to experience the hand of another presence in my affairs. When you walk in the woods and suddenly come across a footprint, at first you can marvel at the shape and clarity of the print. But you know it was a print and not something that grows out of the ground by itself. It is caused by the passing of some creature. You look at it and as you consider its various aspects, the shape of an animal begins to form in your mind. You see in your mind's eye a raccoon, or a deer or whatever coincides with the print in the earth.

That's how I began to see the turning points in my life and how the various event prints began to take shape. How was it that I happened to stop to cross at a red light in New York City and while I waited, happened to look into the wastebasket? I don't usually look into wastebaskets and if I do I don't normally read what's in them. There was the open newspaper with a message blaring at me as if printed just for my benefit that day. I had never heard of consulting before. Why should it grab my interest? It was an aggressive ad and normally would turn me off. Not this time. It piqued my interest and I phoned the number. How is it that I became so leery of the interviewer and eventually of the organization? Was it that warning bells were sounding in me?

How was it I happened to find the Association of Consulting Engineers? Doesn't this begin to look like the actions of a determined person? It is beginning to look as though I knew exactly what I was doing, but I didn't. Why did the man at the Association offer so much help? Why did he connect me with the Vice President who became my mentor? Why did I become more and more interested in a profession I knew nothing about? Isn't it amazing that Barrington and Company just landed that assignment in time for me to apply? Why did they offer me the job; surely not because I knew how to teach? Why would the Vice President take so much interest in me and devote so much of his energy and time to teach me everything he knew about consulting?

Why? Questions upon questions led me along. This chain of coincidental events is colored through and through with other influences than mine. A presence was at work beyond my consciousness. I only asked why, because I didn't see the causes of these events. Coincidence can describe what we don't know of these events but it is not satisfying. I really wanted to know the causes, the invisible causes intervening and influencing everything others and I did. Not in a thousand years could I have arranged all the intricate choreography that accounted for that turning point in my life. We like to think that such events are simply accidental or coincidental. However, what help are those words? They simply are a convenient term employed to label something we don't know which eases our worry about the unknown and puts our curiosity to rest.

I urge each of you to revisit your own turning points and look for the unseen presence, the hand or footprints of the benign companions that labor invisibly in our biographies side by side with us. I could give countless examples out of my own life. How I met my wife for instance. Did I choreograph her migrations through Switzerland, Germany, England, and the United States to the point where we met in New York City? I am not that smart! After fifty years of our life together, many children, professional achievements and companionship, I can only look at the delicate prints in the choreography of my life with immense gratitude and respect. Somebody is interested in my endeavors. I have an unseen partner whose prints are left all over my biography.

56. Spirit and Matter

Through this process of investigation into my biography I came to know my Angel. It is an intimate relationship. Sometimes I search for her presence, sometimes she takes the liberty to intervene unasked because long ago we have developed an understanding that her involvement in my life is desired and always welcome. Occasionally, especially when I was younger, I blundered ahead briefly without taking her indications to heart. As a result I have a few turns in my life that feel like detours. Did my Angel abandon me for my thick-headedness? Not at all! It seems we need each other. Sometimes when I am feeling particularly pleased with myself I wonder whether I am actually contributing to my Angel's development as well. Such a wonderful working together on so many levels must be mutually beneficial in some way. Perhaps this spirit partner—never wholly revealed to me, but always present as I think, feel, and act in the world—is joined to me with an intense karma that endures over more than one lifetime. I would not be surprised if that turns out to be true.

So how do we change? Not alone, certainly. We change in the company of others, both human and invisible. We change rapidly when we invite connections with those who intersect with our biographies. Another way to put it might be to say our biographies cannot be created solo. Whoever gets involved with us becomes a co-creator of our biography. Invisible and visible partners co-create our biography with us as a work of art to be set aside one day at the end of our lives with its essences imbedded in our souls for future lifetimes.

Bearing in mind these delicate spiritual connections for each of us, RSF began to change the way the world works with money. It has achieved some modest success. The success is not because its management and staff are cleverer than others are and not because they have unique ideas or better visions than others do.

The success is due largely to three major factors:

1. Respect for what lives in many human beings as initiative and spiritual striving,
2. Willingness to cultivate relationships as a basis for structuring and managing meaningful monetary transactions, and
3. Exhibiting the courage to invite the spirit of our time into our daily activity, fostering paths of development that connect the spirit in each of us with the spirit in the universe.

To learn more about RSF you can log on to the web site to discover how the organization is able to do this work.

57. THE PRESENT

Moving from the example of RSF to our personal stories let's examine what we have discovered. We have explored a number of situations in story form and looked more deeply into the nature of money, its role in our culture and its spiritual significance because we want to bring healing forces into the movement of money. These stories and many others like it have brought me to a number of basic conclusions as follows: The nature of money is bound up with the nature of the human being, the stage of development at which we find ourselves, and the form of consciousness we currently possess. All of these have a history through which the evolution of money weaves like a golden thread in a tapestry.

In section one, we considered employing a more creative kind of thinking I call imaginative thinking to delve behind the sense perceptible phenomena into the invisible world of causes that we uncover through such thinking.

In sections two, three, and four, we explored the nature of money by experiencing in story form how the three transaction types move money and give it certain qualitative attributes. We learn that money is only money during an actual transaction and in so doing aligns itself with the invisible world of the soul and spirit in every human being. Whatever we don't like about the movement of money in society has its root causes in our behavior and actions.

In section five, we determined how capital arose through the insertion of the human intellect into our labor and how so much of the human spirit has been devoted almost exclusively to pampering our physical needs. We considered the proposition that humanity is waking up to its spiritual core and beginning to take responsibility for what happens between us and on the earth.

Section six asked: Who is this party to every transaction, the so-called individuality present in many human beings? How did it come about in the course of evolutionary history or rather *Ourstory,* and where are we now? I asked that we consider ethical individualism as the natural consequence of individuality espousing altruism as its mode of functioning in the future.

Section seven presented the example of RSF, how karma choreographed the gathering of the founders and the initial support it gained. Also considered was the connection of the spiritual RSF with the legal and material RSF and that the spiritual RSF was already at work many years before it materialized for sense perception.

In section eight, we opened up the potential in our future, how money and we develop and are inextricably bound together. Money is our instrument for supporting ethical individualism.

We now need to consider what steps we can take to develop further our human nature that is the invisible cause for the movement of money.

The nature of the human being is threefold. We live in a physical form that has gone through the longest evolutionary process. What we see of each other with our senses is ancient. All scientists, religious leaders, scriptures agree on this point, that humans did not spring fully formed from a conch shell, but developed over eons of time. It took eons of time to evolve the human physical entity to the perfection it now enjoys. The physical body, composed largely of liquids, is an engineering marvel that includes the miracle of life and the windows of our senses toward the world from which we enrich our feeling life. The capacity to think, to feel, and to will are supported by this physical instrument each of us inherits through our ancestors.

We are also endowed with a soul that develops over time through many incarnations. Imbedded in the soul are the residue of previous experiences, relationships and inclinations, which play into our current consciousness and bring us in mysterious ways to fulfill our deepest intentions. We long to perfect ourselves and develop all that is in our nature to become. Our abilities to think, feel, and will are forces residing in the soul, ready to serve others and us.

During the last several thousand years, something else has been added to our nature that is unseen, that cannot be ascertained through the senses, and whose existence cannot be proven. Present in each of us is our individuality, something we can refer to as "I." It is a wonderful word that each of us can only use in referring to ourselves. "I" has only one meaning, even though there are as many examples of it as there are human beings. If we are not sure we have it, we will in time as we develop. Only someone who has experienced their own individuality can prove its existence to himself or herself. No arguments or external demonstrations will either verify or invalidate its existence. We who work upright between heaven and earth now have the spirit intended in our origins within us.

Once there were the gods and we were in our infancy. Then the gods retreated into temples and churches and then left us altogether to find what is new in each of us. The god in us now lives. What happens from now on depends on us. We have been given all we need to take charge of all that has been given us. It is this spirit active within the human soul that can be responsible for the movement of money. If this upright spirit in us controls our transactional activity, only good will come of it. Every transaction is a social event, for all its myriad variations. It cannot happen internally, only externally between two parties. The human spirit engages with others to transact events which provide the global, circulatory movement we call money.

When the movement of money is rapid, young in character, we call it buying/ selling. This is one aspect of the monetary circulatory system. At this stage it supports all that we need for life on earth. Whatever we buy stimulates the whole world economy to produce the same product or service again. It is our responsibility to buy what we would like the world to produce for us. For example, if we purchase fair trade organic coffee we encourage others to follow suit and we support farmers and give them a decent living.

When the movement of money slows down, eddies in small pools and ages, we call it lending/borrowing. At this stage money engages each of us in the karma of the past and in forming new karmic connections for the future. The banking profession as it currently exists tries to mask this reality. It is uncomfortable to include karma in our lending practices so banks bury it in a kind of mock objectivity. In the future, banking will adopt its intended role of regulating the movement of money so that it serves individuals in fulfilling their destinies and the choreography of intentional communities arising and dissolving in accordance with their purposes. It is our responsibility to bring soul into our lending/borrowing so that all humans are empowered to fulfill their destinies. When RSF lends to a young initiative under the right conditions, individuals group together to fulfill a dream they share. The

RSF was created to enable those intending to imbue the movement of money with soul power, to work together collaboratively.

When the movement of money dies and fades out of the economy, only to support the spiritual/cultural life of our society, renewing us and refreshing us for our responsibilities and tasks, we call it giving/receiving. These transactions incorporate into our society what first lives in our souls as imaginations. When a school community, serving young children, needs a classroom, the gift that makes it possible lives on in the school and eventually realizes its full value many years later. The children whom it first benefited may be long gone, as might be the teachers and the parents as well as the donors. Gifts live on beyond the donors. They transform the world into what we can imagine it to be. It is our responsibility to cherish imaginations that are uplifting and progressive so that our giving/receiving entices the highest possible ideals into existence.

In the future, as the human being matures and evolves further toward its natural altruistic nature, the circulatory system of money in our human social life will be kept healthy through the incorporation of the highest human ideals into its movement around the globe. We will feel obligated to support each other, recognizing that supporting any one of us helps all of us. We will not be able to bear the want or suffering of any other soul. It will be so obvious to us that the harm any one of us endures lames every other one of us. Money will no longer be an object, but a sustaining worldwide movement regulated by our higher selves and a means to provide support to empower each other toward deeds for the good in all of us.

58. THE BEGINNING

IN CONCLUSION, WE have before us two challenges. One is the challenge to work on ourselves and the other challenge is to work on how we deal with money. Let's take first what we can do to work on ourselves, and then consider how we can work with money to connect our values with the movement of money.

To develop our own capacities there are three crucial exercises we can practice. They are all simple to do. Anyone can practice them and no special skill is required. Only determination to practice them is needed.

The first exercise is, once every day, practice thinking imaginatively about something you observe. It can be a stone, a plant, an animal, or a person. Explore penetrating through your sense perception to discover the invisible ideas and concepts that are inherent in the object you are observing. Don't fantasize or lose yourself in playful imaginings. Stick with your perceptions and let your thinking penetrate to the invisible reality behind the sense impressions. Notice how each object reveals something unique to you. The invisible causes behind our world of effects reveal themselves to us. Practice sensing the invisible in all things visible. This will develop your imaginative cognition and increasingly connect you with the invisible causes working behind our normal sense impressions. You will get used to looking into the invisible unknown for causes of the effects you perceive.

The second exercise is, once every week, feel what's going on in your own soul. This requires a little more time and determination, but it should be possible to do at least once a week. Ask yourself, "What do I feel?" You may draw a blank to begin with, or you may insert something into your soul that you are thinking, without realizing that's what you are doing. Feelings do not have names. That is a thought coming from the head, which likes to organize feelings into categories. A pure feeling is absolutely unique. It has never occurred before nor will it ever occur again because it is pure internal sensation.

You will discover, as I did, that it doesn't really belong to you, nor is it an objective part of the world. It exists between you and the world, as if you and the world are co-creators of the unique sensation you feel. It tells you something about yourself and it tells you something about the world, but it never gets as crystal clear as a thought. You're dying to think, but resist the temptation and continue to live entirely within the feeling as long as you can.

It is helpful for this exercise if you practice it in a quiet, peaceful place to begin with. I have done it in the midst of a noisy crowd, although it is harder and requires a stronger power of concentration. This exercise teaches us how to observe the ebb and flow of our feeling life that accompanies everything we think and do. After a while we will be aware of our feelings as a kind of harmony to the conscious melody of our thoughts and deeds.

The third exercise is, once every month at least, to pour your whole soul into something you decide to do. It could be as simple as doing the dishes after a meal. Really do the work well, so well that it has never been done before with such intense determination to make it the best dishwashing the world has ever seen. It could also be more complicated like weeding a flower or vegetable bed in your garden. If you are like me, your whole soul is, at first, bent on getting it over with as quickly as possible. Resist that temptation and regard it as something that will change the world if your entire being is represented in it. Change the whole world by pouring all of your body, soul, and spirit into the point in the universe where you are. Feel how you become a transformer of reality. Pour out all that you have to ensoul existence with your presence. This exercise will help to develop a unified presence in life of body, soul, and spirit.

From my experience in life over the past seventy-four years, these three exercises are the most important activity any one of us can undertake regularly and with determination. They will begin a unique process of actualizing the unique presence of body, soul, and spirit that makes us human. I can give no better advice to anyone. Each one of these exercises will lead to consequences in your soul and before you know it, you will be on a path of development. Standing still in your soul will begin to feel uncomfortable. You will be moving internally the way money moves externally. Your inner motion, along self-determined pathways, always requires your willed effort, but you will be assisted as you move. That's been my experience and I treasure movement in my soul.

We also want to practice certain exercises to increase our healing effect on the movement of money. These exercises are also simple if practiced regularly and with determination. They are based on having read and digested the content of this book and require only a willingness to grant that we have gained some deeper understanding of monetary transactions and want them to have a healing influence on the world. Again these exercises are three in number, can be practiced by absolutely anyone who wants to. There is no entrance examination for this schooling. No special skills are demanded. It helps to be aware of many insights in this book, but even if you have not read this book, you can still practice these three exercises and succeed in achieving a more active connection with your money.

The first exercise is to pause in your buying and penetrate through to your motive and connection with the object of your desire. This moment of pausing can be rich with inner experience about yourself and why you are buying and reveal the nature of your desires. Feel your participation in a rapid current of exchange and your creation of a value that sends a message to the entire world economy about the nature of your soul. I am assuming that you are generally buying thoughtfully. You are buying only what you want the world to produce or grow. You are making sure no one is made to suffer, either children or adults, in order to satisfy your desire. You are checking to see whether producing or growing what you desire is not harming or poisoning the earth as a living organism. You are buying with a social conscience. This exercise is one that will help you to do that. It develops the soul muscles to buy as a whole, conscious being.

The second exercise is, every now and then, to identify those to whom you might be willing to lend money. The important question is not how much or why, but who! *Who* is the most important question when it comes to borrowing and lending. Discover with whom you are connected by asking this question. You can also broaden the question and ask what organization would you want to borrow from, or what organization would you want to invest in and trust they will safely do the most good with your money? You may discover that you don't want to know who or what will be done with your money. You may want to keep it impersonal and hidden from your conscience as it may be too uncomfortable to look at in this way. This exercise will lead to further self-knowledge and further awakening so that one day when you really need to borrow, or when you are ready to invest consciously, you will at least have other options from which to choose. Every time you borrow or lend you are dealing with past and future karma and the life of soul.

If you are ready to really care what your money is doing in the world, consider investing in RSF. Find out about the South Shore Bank in Chicago, or the New Century Bank in Kimberton, Pennsylvania, or the New Resource Bank in San Francisco or any of the other socially constructive banks. One way to learn more is to read the *Quarterly News* from RSF and read about projects that your money can help to support.

The third exercise is, whenever the spirit moves you, to give consciously with full awareness that you are really inserting spirit into reality and incarnating whatever lives in your imagination for the future. We give all the time, to our children, our churches, mosques, and synagogues. Giving is quite natural. It is in our nature. Every time we give, we are dealing with spirit in one way or another. We are either fostering a child's development, a facility in which spiritual renewal can take place, or supporting any one of our noblest of cultural achievements, such as music, art, or dance. Know that when you give, and every time you give, you are drawing spiritual impulses into the world that will change it.

These are the three personal exercises and the three exercises in real life pertaining to the movement of money I can heartily recommend anyone to try. They will awaken you further to the magic in money. I believe that those who do them qualify themselves to move money and to participate as a leader in the progress of our social life. The exercises are only a beginning, a place to start. To start means to move inwardly along a new path. You will be walking the talk along a path that reveals additional steps along the way.

Money as circulatory movement that carries value in its energy has the potential to transform and heal our personal selves as well as our social field, the field in which we meet each other and transact creative business. People as the transactors who move money in partnership imbue the movement of money with healing forces that will cure our social ills.

Is all of this revolutionary? I do not think so. I believe it already lives in us, already exists in germinal form in our very nature and in our connection with the spirit in the world. The spirit in the world seeks us without forcing us. The spirit in us seeks the spirit in the world without loss of freedom and independent initiative. All of our present institutions will change, not as currently apprehended, but as currently verifiable in the social movements of our time. RSF has initiated conferences in which successful business leaders are creating businesses that are designed to further human health, a healthy environment, and a healthy working culture. I meet business leaders right now who already exemplify the future role of business in our society. I have met educators who are seeing how wrong our present view of education is and are working to transform it. Stuffing information into children is not educating them. Education means drawing out of children what is there as potential. The rightful role of education is to ease the entry into our present cultural epoch and preserve in all children the new social impulses brought into the stream of their lives.

The healing force in our culture is the moving circulation of money that touches all things, all humans, and all the visible artifacts in our cultural setting. It is we who give the movement of money its healing powers. Each one of us is a physician in residence on the earth. As has been said, "Physician, heal thyself!" So must it be said of us. We, human beings, responsible for what happens on our watch, must begin by healing ourselves and then using money to heal the world. Healing means to wake up and act responsibly. Buy and sell only what we want the world to produce. Lend to and borrow from socially constructive organizations that seek the further development of the human being and support initiative taking that is socially constructive. Give to and receive to accomplish a rich cultural life that welcomes humanity into incarnation on the earth and provides a life for each of us that enriches and encourages our whole being.

Money and we are wedded as the world and we are wedded. What we can determine consciously will undoubtedly have some effect on what happens in the future. Whatever we do not determine consciously is likely to open a space for unknown determinants. Such determinants are likely to be both beneficial as well as detrimental. Whichever they are, we are left out of the action, placidly on the receiving end of unknown forces.

Our money is money only when it is in motion through transactions. If you and I plan to be responsible beings conscious of our affect on life, we need to enter into every transaction with full awareness of subsequent as well as previous connections. Changing the world for the better begins with us. It will not happen by itself. It requires us to begin somewhere and do it. My hope is that the six exercises I have proposed will entice a number of readers to make such a beginning.

As stated at the introduction of this book, *Money Can Heal* is a call to the social physicians of every race, religion, nation, and gender that wish to heal our social life. It is a call to those who want to let their finest forces stream into the realm of reality in a manner that positively affects our monetary circulation.

We are the beginning of all healing; money will follow our lead.

SIEGFRIED FINSER is available for lectures, workshops, and advice. He may be contacted by email at sigfin@juno.com.

NOTES

INTRODUCTION

1. The bibliography lists a number of such books, which the reader will find stimulating and challenging, especially as the writers apply many of the ideas contained in their books in their practical work and professions.
2. Rudolf Steiner, *Intuitive Thinking as a Spiritual Path: A Philosophy of Freedom,* Great Barrington, MA: SteinerBooks, 1994.

1. IMAGINATION AND MONEY

1. Edward Lee Thorndike, *Educational Psychology: Briefer Course,* New York: Teacher's College, Columbia University, 1910.
2. Jack Weatherford, *The History of Money,* Three Rivers Press, 1997; Glyn Davies, *A History of Money: From Ancient Times to the Present Day,* Cardiff: University of Wales Press, 2002.
3. M. Dorothy Belgrave and Hilda Hart, *Norse Myths*, (Smithmark Publishers, n.d.).
4. Paul Einzig, *Primitive Money in Its Ethnological, Historical, and Economic Aspects,* 2d ed., New York: Pergamon Press, 1966, 15.

3. BORROWING AND LENDING

1. The Grameen Foundation is a nonprofit organization whose goal is to use microfinance and innovative technology to fight global poverty and provide opportunities to the world's poorest people. With tiny loans, financial services, and technology, they help the poor, mostly women, initiate self-sustaining businesses. The organization operates a global network of microfinance partners in twenty-two countries. See Muhammad Yunus, *Banker to the Poor: Micro-Lending and the Battle against World Poverty,* New York: Perseus Books, 1999.

5. OUR SOCIAL LIFE WITH OTHERS

1. The Threefold Educational Foundation, founded in 1926, supports anthroposophic initiatives in education, the arts, agriculture, and community building.

2. For further study, read Rudolf Steiner, *The Renewal of the Social Organism* (Great Barrington, MA: Anthroposophic Press, 1985), which contains articles and essays on his discovery of what he calls the "threefold social organism."

6. Our Evolving Consciousness

1. Belgrave and Hart, *Norse Myths*. (Smithmark).
2. Ibid.
3. Homer, *Iliad*, trans. Rouse.
4. Finser, Siegfried E., *The Last King of Rome*, Windrose Series #6002, Copyright © 1995, Rose Harmony Association Inc., Chaham, New York.
5. For more information, see Titus Livy, *Livy: Early History of Rome;* see *Plutarch's Lives* for references to all of the seven kings; see Cicero, *The Republic*, which describes the early founding of Rome and the seven kings.
6. For a thorough and stimulating discussion of ethical individualism, consult *The Philosophy of Spiritual Activity* by Rudolf Steiner. This book also appears under the titles *Intuitive Thinking as a Spiritual Path* and as *The Philosophy of Freedom*.

7. The Example of RSF

1. *Anthroposophy* is the name Rudolf Steiner gave to the ongoing effort to bring soul and spirit into human consciousness and action. I have been a student of Steiner's work ever since my teens. For those interested in learning more about this philosophy see the bibliography.

8. The Future

1. Rudolf Steiner, *Verses & Meditations,* Rudolf Steiner Press, 1993, pg. 117.
2. Goethe, *The Green Snake and the Beautiful Lily*, SteinerBooks, 2006.
3. Edward Lee Thorndike published in 1918 The nature, purpose, and general methods of measrements of educational products in chapter 2 in G. M. Whipple (ed.). *The Seventeenth yearbook of the National Society for Study of Education,* part 2, p. 16. presumed by many that this proposition 6 as well as proposition 7 restates R. Descartes ideas in the *Principles of Philosophy* (1644), II:64.
4. René Descartes, *Principles of Philosophy* (1644), II:64.

BIBLIOGRAPHY

Belgrave, Dorothy M. and Hart, Hilda, *Norse Myths*, Anness Publishing Ltd., 1996, This edition published by Smithmark Publishers, a division of U.S. Media Holdings, San Francisco, 2001.

De Graaf, James, Thomas H. Naylor, and David Wann, *Affluenza: The All-Consuming Epidemic*, Berrett-Koehler Publishers, San Francisco, 2001.

Galbraith, John Kenneth, *Economics in Perspective: A Critical History*, Houghton Mifflin, Boston, 1987.

Homer, *Iliad,* W. H. D. Rouse, trans., Heron, London, 1969.

Kelly, Marjorie, *The Divine Right of Capital: Dethroning the Corporate Aristocracy*, Berrett-Koehler, San Francsco, 2001.

Kennedy, Margrit and Declan Kennedy, *Interest and Inflation Free Money: Creating an Exchange Medium That Works for Everybody and Protects the Earth*, revised ed., New Society Publishers, Philadelphia, 1995.

Kinder, George, *Seven Stages of Money Maturity: Understanding the Spirit and Value of Money in Your Life,* Delacorte Press, New York, 1999.

Lietaer, Bernard, *The Future of Money: Creating New Wealth, Work, and a Wiser World,* Random House, New York, 2001.

Lietaer, Bernard, and Stephen M. Belgin, *Of Human Wealth*. Galley Edition, Boulder, CO, 2004.

Mellon, Theodore J., *The Journey Toward Masterful Philanthropy*. Five Centuries Press, Boulder, CO, 2004.

Steiner, Rudolf, *Economics: The World as One Economy*, New Economy Publications, London, 1972.

———, *Education As a Force for Social Change,* Anthroposophic Press, Great Barrington, MA, 1997.

Twist, Lynne, *The Soul of Money: Transforming Your Relationship with Money and Life,* Norton, New York, 2003.

Weatherford, Jack, *The History of Money*. Three Rivers Press, New York, 1997.

Yunus, Muhammad, *Banker to the Poor: Micro-Lending and the Battle Against World Poverty,* PublicAffairs, New York, 2003.

ALSO FROM STEINERBOOKS:

ORGANIZATIONAL INTEGRITY
How to Apply the Wisdom of the Body
to Develop Healthy Organizations

by Torin Finser, author of
School as a Journey • *School Renewal* • *In Search of Ethical Leadership*

ALL AROUND, WE see living systems in plants, animals, and human beings. Our environment is alive, vibrant, and full of innate wisdom. Even the stars and planets speak in ancient folklore to those who have ears to hear. Our very lives depend on this interdependence and the myriad connections that surround us. Nonetheless, many people experience organizations as inert, bureaucratic, inflexible obstacles to innovation and human initiative. People have struggled for years to survive the weight of apathy in organizations such as large school systems, corporations, and government agencies such as FEMA.

Organic Organizations attempts to reclaim and reconcile organizational dynamics with living systems. The wisdom found in human organs, minerals, planets, and even sacred geometry is used to reinvent organizations. Organizations are supposed to serve, and their forms and structures need to mirror the living systems of those who have come together with common purpose. We need to change our ideas of organizations and establish a new paradigm so that future organizations will be worthy of the people in them.

We need a new ecology of organizations. It is time for a new revolution that creates dynamic, living organizations by the people and for the people. Just as democracy has transformed much of the world, we can use the genius of the body to reform organizations into living systems that serve and protect human interests.

⋅⇒ ⇐⋅

TORIN M. FINSER, PH.D., is Director of Waldorf Teacher Training at Antioch New England Graduate School and founding member of the Center for Anthroposophy, Collaborative Leadership Training and Templar Associates in New Hampshire. He has been an educator for nearly three decades and has consulted with public and Waldorf schools in areas of facilitating change, designing mentoring and evaluation programs, and, more recently, leadership mentoring.

IN FINE BOOKSTORES AND FROM STEINERBOOKS — WWW.STEINERBOOKS.ORG